THE
SHRED
DIET
COOKBOOK

Also by Ian K. Smith, M.D.

THE SHRED DIET COOKBOOK

Ian K. Smith, M.D.

ST. MARTIN'S PRESS ≈ NEW YORK

www.stmartins.com

Library of Congress Cataloging-in-Publication Data

Smith, Ian, 1969–
    The shred diet cookbook / Ian K. Smith, M.D. — First edition.
        pages cm
ISBN 978-1-250-06121-8 (hardcover)
ISBN 978-1-4668-6685-0 (e-book)
1. Reducing diets — Recipes.
2. Weight loss. I. Title.
  RM222.2.S626 2015
  641.5'63—dc23

                          2014040247

St. Martin's Press books may be purchased for educational, business, or promotional use. For information on bulk purchases, please contact the Macmillan Corporate and Premium Sales Department at 1-800-221-7945, extension 5442, or write to specialmarkets@macmillan.com.

First Edition: March 2015

10 9 8 7 5 4 3 2 1

To Dashiell and Declan, the two best little chefs in our house, whose creativity and recipes keep us smiling and satisfied at the dinner table.

CONTENTS

ACKNOWLEDGMENTS

A book of this scope has a lot of moving parts that readers never see. There are many in the process who work hard to help turn my creative vision into a reality. Pressing deadlines, tight shoot dates, artistic conundrums—there are a lot of demands that need to be met to produce what you are about to enjoy. The names that follow might not be recognizable to you, but they are extremely important to me and the members of the team. I want them to know how much they're appreciated and to honor their diligence and assistance. Thanks to my home team—Tristé, Dash, and Declan—for all of your recipe ideas, sampling, and patience. My mother, Rena, Aunt Lynn, and Uncle Johnny generously explained some of our family's favorite recipes. Editorial and artistic greatness came from: Elizabeth Beier, Michelle Richter, Anya Lichtenstein, Steve Cohen, John Karle, Sally Richardson, Jen Enderlin, George Witte, and Crystal Ben. Marketing savvy team members were: Stephanie Davis, Jeanne-Marie Hudson, and Marie Estrada. Big thanks to Rachael Ray, who after working with me for years gave me the courage to take on the kind of project she always makes look so easy on her television shows. I am grateful for recipe masters Wes Martin and Chris Peterson, great photographer Ben Fink and his team, and last but not least, the awesome SHREDDERS who keep SHREDDER Nation growing and thriving and losing weight: Bev Simon, Sandra Chiasson, Felicia Tate, Wendi Keathley, Becky Barnes, Missy Thacket-Warner, and Lori Clark Warner.

INTRODUCTION

Eating good food is a pleasure that we all should enjoy. Sometimes the best foods are simplest and don't need to be prepared by a renowned chef or in a fully gourmet kitchen. Great meals should be something that all of us can create in our own kitchens, regardless of our culinary talents, time, or resources. I decided to write *The SHRED Diet Cookbook* because I like food, but I *love* good food. I want to prove that healthy food can be fun and tasty and satisfying.

Hundreds of thousands of people around the world are part of SHREDDER Nation, a diverse community of SHREDDERs who believe that losing weight and maintaining weight does not mean you must be relegated to a diet of carrots and celery. Sitting down to a good meal is something to look forward to and an opportunity to try new flavors and food combinations. Whether you are following one of the SHRED plans or not, these recipes are enjoyable.

In this fast-paced, over-connected world, we tend to ignore some of the things that really count, and delicious food is at the top of the list. I wanted to assemble a group of recipes that can help you lose weight but would never be considered diet food. What would life be without pancakes, pizza, and good barbecue? Make these recipes with pride, and eat your creations with unabashed pleasure.

Cheers,
Ian K. Smith, M.D.
March 2015

EATING THE SHRED WAY

SHRED and SUPER SHRED are more than just popular diet programs; they are a way of life. When I envisioned these programs, I had three rules in mind. First, they must be inexpensive. Second, they must be realistic. Third, they must not ask for perfection. With these three cornerstones as a foundation, the SHRED lifestyle was born. So many SHREDDERs have emailed, tweeted, or posted Facebook messages saying they would like a cookbook of SHRED-approved meals that would help them continue to lose weight while at the same time not compromising taste. People who are trying to lose weight want to have fun, delicious meals just like everyone else, maybe more than everyone else. Getting banished to the diet aisle in the grocery store is no one's idea of a good time. *The SHRED Diet Cookbook* is my scrumptious answer to your desire to eat great food and lose weight.

What many SHREDDERs find appealing is that the foods that are suggested on the programs are real, affordable foods that you can find in almost any grocery store. There are plenty of tasty, healthy foods that are not organic or carrying some barely unpronounceable name. Many of the foods that we've been eating since we were children are completely acceptable, but SHRED teaches you how to prepare them in a healthier way so that they don't lose their flavor and their calorie counts don't add unwanted pounds.

The idea that a person might live the rest of their life without having a slice of pizza is crazy. Pizza, burgers, and pasta are fun, tasty foods that also can be quite nutritious depending on how they're prepared and the size of the portions. It is only realistic to expect that people are going to have these foods as well as ice cream and cake and other favorites. The SHRED lifestyle doesn't ban these foods, nor does it punish you for having them. Instead, it teaches you how to literally have your cake and eat it too. You'll satisfy your craving, but at the same time not increase those numbers on the scale. Everything in moderation is really something that a SHREDDER can live by as long as the balance leans toward clean, healthy eating.

Although many believe that losing weight means a strict diet of whole grains, fiber, and super foods, the truth of the matter is that no one is nor can be expected to be perfect when it comes to making nutrition and exercise decisions. Sometimes the portion might be bigger than suggested. You might have a couple of glasses of wine instead of one. You might not make it to the gym to work out on your scheduled day. The SHRED lifestyle acknowledges that you will not be perfect. SHRED and SUPER SHRED don't penalize you for being human.

SHRED: The Revolutionary Diet is the original program that works in six-week cycles. After completing the six weeks, you cycle back and do another six weeks but in a different sequence. The program is based on three major components: spacing out your meals; eating four small- to moderate-sized meals a day; and diet confusion for which you vary the types and quantity of foods. The average results from this six-week program are 20 pounds, 4 inches, and two sizes. Although the timing of meals and snacks can be different for everyone based on when you get up to start your day, a typical eating day on the SHRED program might look something like this:

8:30 A.M.	10:00 A.M.	11:30 A.M..	1:00 P.M.	3:30 P.M.	7:00 P.M.	8:30 P.M.
Meal 1	Snack 1	Meal 2	Snack 2	Meal 3	Meal 4	Snack 3

This is an example of what day 1 week 2 on SHRED might look like:

MEAL 1

- 1 banana
- Smoked Salmon and Egg Sandwich (page 29)
- ½ cup of apple juice (*not* from concentrate)

SNACK 1

- Artichoke-Basil Dip and Celery (page 275)

MEAL 2

- 1 cup of Smoky Lentil Soup (page 67)

- Unlimited plain water (flat or fizzy)

SNACK 2

- Mediterranean Popcorn (page 278)

MEAL 3

- Small green garden salad (Only 3 tablespoons of fat-free dressing, no bacon bits, no croutons. Keep it clean.)
- Herbed Goat Cheese–Stuffed Chicken Breasts with steamed broccoli (page 193)
- 1 cup of unsweetened iced tea

MEAL 4

- 1 bowl of Tomato and White Bean Soup (page 70)
- 1 serving of Simple, Gorgeous Glazed Carrots (page 272)
- 1 cup of lemonade and 1 cup of plain water

SNACK 3

- Smoky Kale Chips (page 282)

SUPER SHRED: The Big Results Diet is the accelerated version of *SHRED*. This is a program designed for people who want to lose weight quickly, but in a healthy manner. Many who have reached a weight-loss plateau or who need to get the weight off quickly because they are going on vacation or have an event to attend soon will use this four-week accelerated program. The average result after these four weeks is an astounding 20-pound weight loss. Some people will do a cycle of SHRED, then a cycle of SUPER SHRED and all types of combinations, mixing up the routine to keep their weight loss going.

SUPER SHRED's primary concepts are **Negative Energy Balance** (energy consumed is less than the energy expended), **Calorie Disruption** (varying the quantity of calories you consume each day), and **Sliding Nutrient Density** (eating more plant-based meals during the latter part of the day). Each of the four weeks of SUPER SHRED is dramatically different, but here is what a typical day of week 1 might look like:

7:30 A.M.	8:30 A.M.	10:00 A.M.	11:30 A.M.	12:30 A.M.	4:30 P.M.	7:30 P.M.
Awake	Meal 1	Snack 1	Snack 2	Meal 2	Meal 3	Meal 4

This is an example of what day 1 week 1 on SUPER SHRED might look like:

MEAL 1

- ½ cup of blueberries
- 1 cup of apple-walnut grits
- 1 cup of fresh orange juice or 1 cup of coffee (limit sugar to 1 packet; limit milk or half-and-half to 1 tablespoon)

SNACK 1

- Mexican Pita Chips (page 270)

SNACK 2

- 1 bag of White Cheddar SHRED POP popcorn™ (www.shredlife.com)

MEAL 2

- Vigorous Green Smoothie (page 302)

MEAL 3

- Bowl of Uncle Johnny's Black-Eyed Pea Salad (page 14)
- 1 cup of lemonade

MEAL 4

- Start with 1 cup of water
- Grilled Garlic-Lemon Sea Bass (page 188) and steamed vegetables
- 1 cup unsweetened iced tea

The core of the SHRED lifestyle is also the core of *The SHRED Diet Cookbook*. These recipes are meant to be fun, tasty, healthy, easy, and satisfying. Some of the recipes are simplified, healthier versions of old standards, whereas others will have ingredients that you might not have tried before and that will open your palate to something new and wonderful. Just like the SHRED diet programs, I have arranged this book to be easy and to the point. If you're following one of the programs, you might alter a recipe to fit the recommendations for a calorie count for that particular meal. There are lots of creative, tasty recipes in this book, so be adventurous and try out as many of them as possible. Some you will eventually identify as your go-to recipes; others you might decide to save for special occasions when you want something unique and satisfying. The bottom line is that you don't have to be a James Beard Award–winning chef to cook and enjoy these recipes. You simply need an open mind, a few ingredients, a few well-used pots and pans, and a willingness to have fun. Enjoy!

BREAKFAST RECIPES

2

Energy Blast Yogurt

Healthy Granola

Red Pepper and Scallion Scramble

Pumpkin-Pecan Oatmeal

Grilled Cheese Greatness

Breakfast Quinoa

Herbed Egg-White Wraps

Turkey Sausage Frittata

Whole-Wheat Pancakes with Blueberry-Lemon Compote

Gramma's Old-Fashioned Pancakes

Smoked Salmon and Egg Sandwich

Mediterranean Breakfast Pita Pockets

Individual Mushroom-and-Swiss Quiches

Kale Baked Eggs

Buckwheat Crêpes with Cinnamon Honey

Chia-Pomegranate Breakfast Pudding

Green-Chile-and-Egg Quesadillas

Melon-Berry Cups

Apple-Walnut Grits

Chocolate Whole-Grain Waffles with Strawberry Syrup

Broiled Almond-Banana Toast

A Strong Start to the Day

Breakfast is the most important meal of the day, especially in the SHRED lifestyle. Your body has not been nourished for the last 8 hours and needs to be refueled to start the day. Many make the mistake of thinking that breakfast is a chance to save on calories, so they skip it altogether or they barely eat anything at all.

I like to use a car analogy when I describe the importance of breakfast. Imagine that you've had a busy day driving around running errands and by the time you finally pull into your garage, your car's fuel gauge is just a hair away from being empty. The next day, you have a 200-mile drive planned. Would you hit the road the next morning without getting gas? Of course not. You would refuel first thing so that you have at least enough gas to get to your destination. The same is true of your body's need for fuel in the morning. You need calories and nutrients as a source of fuel to get your day off to a good start.

Make sure you eat breakfast within an hour of getting up. Going too long without nourishment deprives your body and is counterproductive to physical and mental functioning. You will be eating your first snack of the day approximately 90 minutes after having breakfast, so don't wait too late to get in your first meal and throw off the rest of your meal schedule for the day.

Meal spacing can be just as important as what you eat, how much you eat, and the calories you consume. Research has shown that how one spaces their meals can be advantageous to weight loss. Regular eating can have a direct impact on hormones such as insulin and cortisol. These hormones in turn can have an impact on how much and where the body stores fat. Keeping hormone levels as consistent as possible and avoiding spikes in their release as well as their concentration in blood levels can be an added benefit when trying to maintain or lose weight.

The SHRED lifestyle means that there's as much attention paid to *when* you're eating as there is to *what* you're eating. Many people trying to lose weight don't find success because they are not being mindful of when they eat. They go for long periods of time without eating and then indulge in a large meal or snack when they can't take the hunger pains any longer. It's important to avoid this type of sporadic, over-indulgent eating pattern. Distributing calories as evenly as possible throughout the day is an important strategy for optimal nutrition.

The type of fuel you load up on

in the morning is equally important when it comes to creating your best opportunity for a healthy and satisfying day of nourishment. Fiber, protein, and a full complement of vitamins are important when choosing a breakfast in the morning. Ideally, you will want to eat at least five servings of fruits and vegetables combined, so starting the day with one or two servings of fruit is an easy way to make sure you reach this goal on a daily basis. You can eat a piece of fruit as well as a glass of fresh juice or even a smoothie. Don't be afraid to be creative when figuring out a way to get in your fruit.

The following breakfast recipes have been chosen because they check off a lot of boxes. They are easy to prepare, inexpensive, extremely tasty, and pack a powerful nutritional punch. Feel free to make smart substitutions with some of the ingredients, but be mindful of how this might alter the calorie counts as well as other nutritional components of the meal.

ENERGY BLAST YOGURT

The best breakfast to start the day includes fresh, eye-opening flavors that will get you up and moving without making you feel full or setting you up for a midmorning crash. Combining the staying power of oats, a blast of sweetness from fruit and honey, and the pleasing smoothness of yogurt, this one-bowl treat will get you off on the right foot. You can even count on a big helping of antioxidants along with those mouthwatering blueberries!

SERVES 1

One 5.3-ounce container plain nonfat Greek yogurt

½ teaspoon honey

Pinch ground cinnamon

2 tablespoons rolled oats

Zest of 1 lemon

1 tablespoon dried blueberries

1 teaspoon roasted unsalted sunflower seeds

In a small bowl, combine the yogurt, honey, cinnamon, oats, and lemon zest and stir to mix. Let stand about 5 minutes to soften the oats. Sprinkle the blueberries and sunflower seeds over the top and enjoy.

NUTRITIONAL INFORMATION Per Serving: 181 cal., 2 g fat, 0 g sat. fat, 24 g carb., 16 g protein, 70 mg sodium, 10 g sugar, 3 g fiber.

HEALTHY GRANOLA

The name says it all. This is a grab-and-go boost to your immune system, full of usable calories to see you through to lunch without hunger pangs, plus a nice dose of fiber. That's the good news. The better news? All that healthiness comes wrapped in tons of flavor from the nutty almonds, the sweet apple juice, and the sparkle of cinnamon and ginger. It's also a tremendous option as a snack anytime you're in a rush.

1. Preheat the oven to 325 degrees F. Line a baking sheet with parchment paper.

2. Combine the oats, almonds, rice cake, and flaxseed meal in a medium bowl and toss. In another small bowl, whisk together the apple juice, 2 tablespoons of water, the honey, canola oil, vanilla extract, cinnamon, ginger, and salt until combined.

3. Pour the liquid mixture over the dry ingredients and toss well to combine. Spread in a single, even layer on the lined baking sheet.

4. Bake, stirring frequently with a wooden spoon, until golden brown and crisp, about 30 minutes. Remove from the oven, stir in the cranberries, and let stand until completely cool.

5. Serve with yogurt or milk, and store any extra in an airtight container at room temperature.

NUTRITIONAL INFORMATION Per Serving: 301 cal., 8 g fat, 1 g sat. fat, 8 g carb., 8 g protein, 171 mg sodium, 19 g sugar, 4 g fiber.

SERVES 2 (ABOUT 2 CUPS)

1 cup old-fashioned rolled oats

2 tablespoons slivered almonds

1 plain rice cake, crushed into small pieces in a resealable plastic bag

1 tablespoon flaxseed meal

¼ cup apple juice

1 tablespoon honey

2 teaspoons canola oil

½ teaspoon vanilla extract

½ teaspoon ground cinnamon

½ teaspoon ground ginger

Pinch salt

⅓ cup dried cranberries

RED PEPPER AND SCALLION SCRAMBLE

A simple scramble can be a great, protein-rich way to start off your morning, more so if it includes garden-fresh vegetables. The bell peppers and onions perk up the eggs in this dish and are cooked just until they soften so that they go well with the texture of the scramble but not so much that they lose their nutrient value. A little sweet paprika throws in a flavor twist that makes the dish even better.

SERVES 4

2 teaspoons extra-virgin olive oil

½ large red bell pepper, seeded and finely chopped

6 scallions, white and green parts separated and sliced

4 large eggs

4 large egg whites

¼ teaspoon sweet paprika

4 slices whole-grain bread, toasted

2 teaspoons whole-grain mustard

1. Heat the olive oil in a large skillet over medium heat. Add the bell pepper and scallion whites and cook until softened, 3 to 4 minutes. Reduce the heat to medium-low.

2. While they cook, whisk the eggs and egg whites together in a small bowl until combined. Add the paprika, salt and pepper to taste, and whisk to blend.

3. Pour the eggs into the skillet over the bell pepper and onions and cook until the eggs are set and scrambled, 3 to 4 minutes.

4. Spread a thin layer of mustard on each toast slice. Divide the eggs among the toasted bread slices, sprinkle the scallion greens over the top and serve.

NUTRITIONAL INFORMATION Per Serving: 259 cal., 14 g fat, 3 g sat. fat, 21 g carb., 16 g protein, 353 mg sodium, 2 g sugar, 5 g fiber.

Red Pepper and
Scallion Scramble

PUMPKIN-PECAN OATMEAL

Capture the homey comfort of Thanksgiving pumpkin pie in a sturdy breakfast that has cholesterol-beating properties and a nice low fat count by combining canned pumpkin with oatmeal. Spices and nuts give the dish its rich character, but you're sure to be surprised at how well the traditional oats go with the puréed pumpkin. Dessert or breakfast? It'll be hard to tell. Then again, as healthy as this dish is, it doesn't really matter.

SERVES 4

1 cup low-fat milk
½ teaspoon cinnamon
Pinch ground cloves
Pinch salt
¼ cup canned puréed pumpkin
2 tablespoons honey
2 cups old-fashioned rolled oats
⅓ cup chopped toasted pecans
½ teaspoon pure vanilla extract

1. In a large saucepan over medium heat, combine the milk, 1 ½ cups water, cinnamon, cloves, and salt, and bring to a boil.

2. Whisk in the pumpkin and honey until incorporated. Stir in the oats and pecans and simmer, stirring frequently, until the oats are just cooked, 2 to 3 minutes.

3. Remove the pan from the heat, stir in the vanilla extract, and let stand for a few minutes before serving.

NUTRITIONAL INFORMATION Per Serving: 321 cal., 13 g fat, 3 g sat. fat, 44 g carb., 10 g protein, 255 mg sodium, 16 g sugar, 3 g fiber.

Pumpkin-Pecan
Oatmeal

Grilled Cheese
Greatness

GRILLED CHEESE GREATNESS

A plain grilled-cheese sandwich is one of life's simple perfections. It doesn't need to be anything more than it is: just enough cheesy goodness and toasted crunchiness to kill your hunger and satisfy your cravings without splurging big in the calories department. In fact, this treat provides a nice amount of both protein and fiber, thanks to the whole-grain bread. But really, perhaps the most appealing thing about this time-tested kid favorite (and adult favorite too!) is its adaptability; it's the ideal anytime meal when you need a quick, easy, and filling favorite.

1. Spread butter on one side of each slice of bread. Divide the cheese between 2 slices of bread on the nonbuttered side. Top each sandwich with the other slices, buttered-side up.

2. In a large skillet over medium heat, toast the sandwiches for about 5 minutes each side, or until each side is golden brown. Serve hot.

NUTRITIONAL INFORMATION Per Serving: 339 cal., 16 g fat, 8 g sat. fat, 36 g carb., 15 g protein, 446 mg sodium, 6 g sugar, 4 g fiber.

SERVES 2

½ tablespoon unsalted butter, softened

4 slices 100 percent whole-grain bread

½ cup of shredded mild cheddar cheese

BREAKFAST QUINOA

Quinoa is not just for dinner anymore! It actually serves as an incredible alternative to oatmeal, with a subtle, nutty nature and few calories to worry about. Like oatmeal, though, quinoa is the perfect background to some favorite breakfast ingredients, including grapefruit, yogurt, and sweet, sweet orange juice. Pop in a bit of dried ginger and some fresh nutmeg and you have a dynamite breakfast that will give your favorite oatmeal recipe a run for its money.

SERVES 4

1 cup orange juice

¼ teaspoon ground dried ginger

Pinch freshly grated nutmeg

1 cup dried quinoa

1 grapefruit, peeled and segmented

¼ cup nonfat vanilla yogurt

1. In a medium saucepan over medium-high heat, combine the orange juice, 1 cup water, the ginger, and nutmeg and bring to a boil.

2. Stir in the quinoa, reduce the heat to a simmer and cover. Cook until the quinoa has "sprouted" in the pan and absorbed all of the liquid, about 15 minutes.

3. Remove the pan from the heat and divide the quinoa among 4 serving bowls. Top each serving with grapefruit segments and a tablespoon of vanilla yogurt and serve.

NUTRITIONAL INFORMATION Per Serving: 221 cal., 3 g fat, 0 g sat. fat, 43 g carb., 8 g protein, 20 mg sodium, 11 g sugar, 3 g fiber.

HERBED EGG-WHITE WRAPS

Eliminate the yolk of an egg and you're left with a protein-rich white that has little if any fat and cholesterol. Unfortunately, it also has little in the way of flavor, which is why this recipe includes a nice lineup of herbs, a touch of butter, and a little low-fat cheese. Those additions provide sumptuous flavor in a portable serving just right for a breakfast on the go. You won't miss the cholesterol at all.

1. In a medium bowl, combine the egg whites and milk and whisk until frothy and foamy. Add the parsley, chives, and basil and whisk again.

2. Melt the butter in a large nonstick skillet over medium-low heat, swirling to coat the pan. Add the eggs and cook, stirring slowly with a rubber spatula, until the eggs are set, about 5 minutes.

3. Divide the eggs among the tortillas and sprinkle about 1 tablespoon of the cheese over the eggs on each tortilla. Wrap the tortillas, folding in the ends like a burrito. Serve immediately or wrap in aluminum foil to keep warm until ready to eat.

NUTRITIONAL INFORMATION Per Serving: 203 cal., 7 g fat, 3 g sat. fat, 25 g carb., 10 g protein, 475 mg sodium, 0 g sugar, 2 g fiber.

SERVES 4

4 large egg whites

2 tablespoons low-fat milk

2 tablespoons chopped flat-leaf parsley

1 tablespoon chopped fresh chives

6 large basil leaves, finely chopped

1 tablespoon unsalted butter

Four 8-inch whole-wheat tortillas, warmed

¼ cup shredded reduced-fat mozzarella cheese

Turkey Sausage Frittata

TURKEY SAUSAGE FRITTATA

The frittata is the Italian version of the omelet but, oh, so much more. This recipe will save you on those mornings when you're veering dangerously close to popping a couple of frozen waffles in the toaster because you don't have a better idea. Instead, turn to this filling, low-cal, and nutritious option. The addition of turkey sausage gives hearty texture to this meal-in-one.

1. Preheat the oven to 350 degrees F.

2. Heat the olive oil in an 8-inch ovenproof nonstick skillet over medium heat. Add the onion and sausage and cook until the onion is softened and the sausage is cooked through and browned, 6 to 8 minutes. Reduce the heat to low. Spread the sausage and onion out into an even, single layer in the pan.

3. In a small bowl, beat the eggs. Add 2 tablespoons of the parmesan and the salt and pepper and whisk until combined.

4. Slowly pour the eggs over the sausage in the skillet. Let stand for 1 minute until the eggs begins to set on the bottom. Using a large rubber spatula, push the eggs around the edges into the center of the skillet and carefully tilt the pan to allow the liquid eggs to run to the edges of the pan. Sprinkle the remaining 2 tablespoons parmesan evenly over the eggs and transfer the pan to the oven.

SERVES 4

1 teaspoon extra-virgin olive oil

1 small yellow onion, chopped

2 sweet Italian turkey sausages (about 8 ounces total), chopped

6 large eggs

¼ cup grated parmesan, plus more for garnish

Salt and freshly ground black pepper, to taste

1 vine-ripened tomato, seeded and diced

1 teaspoon balsamic vinegar

Continued

5. Cook until the frittata is set and beginning to puff and brown in the center, 10 to 12 minutes.

6. While the frittata cooks, toss the tomatoes with the vinegar in a small bowl. Season with salt and pepper to taste.

7. Remove the skillet from the oven and let stand for about 2 minutes. Using the spatula, release any parts of the frittata that may be stuck to the pan bottom and slide the frittata onto a cutting board or serving plate.

8. Slice the frittata into quarters and top with the marinated tomatoes. Serve with a little more parmesan sprinkled over each slice.

NUTRITIONAL INFORMATION Per Serving: 260 cal., 16 g fat, 6 g sat. fat, 6 g carb., 21 g protein, 409 mg sodium, 3 g sugar, 0 g fiber.

Whole-Wheat Pancakes
with Blueberry-Lemon
Compote

WHOLE-WHEAT PANCAKES

WITH BLUEBERRY-LEMON COMPOTE

Great pancakes don't happen by accident, but get them right and they are heaven on a breakfast plate. These flapjacks get their sturdy character from whole-wheat flour, but they owe their divine flavor to kisses of honey, vanilla, and cinnamon. Compote is just a fancy French word for homemade preserves and a great way to make your own topping without artificial additives. It's so delicious on the pancakes that you may forget the syrup!

1. In a small saucepan over medium heat, combine the blueberries, sugar, and 3 tablespoons water. Bring to a simmer and cook until the blueberries just begin to pop, 3 to 4 minutes. Remove from the heat and stir in the lemon zest. Set aside.

2. In a large bowl, combine the flours, wheat germ, baking powder, cinnamon, and salt. Whisk to incorporate.

3. In a separate large bowl, combine the almond milk, yogurt, eggs, honey, and vanilla extract. Whisk until incorporated. Add the wet ingredients to the dry and stir just until combined. Do not over mix.

4. Coat a large nonstick griddle or skillet with cooking spray and heat over medium heat.

5. Pour ¼ cup of the batter for each pancake on the griddle and cook until bubbles appear on the surface, the edges are set, and the bottom is light golden brown, 2 to 3 minutes. Flip the pancakes and cook until

SERVES 4

For the blueberry-lemon compote:

1 cup fresh blueberries

1 teaspoon granulated sugar

Zest of 1 lemon

For the pancakes:

1 cup whole-wheat flour

½ cup all-purpose flour

¼ cup wheat germ

1 teaspoon baking powder

½ teaspoon ground cinnamon

¼ teaspoon salt

1¼ cups light almond milk

¼ cup nonfat plain Greek yogurt

2 large eggs

1 tablespoon honey

1 teaspoon pure vanilla extract

Cooking spray

Continued

the underside turns golden, about 2 minutes more.

6. Remove the pancakes from the pan and continue with the remaining batter. Serve the pancakes with the compote drizzled over the top.

NUTRITIONAL INFORMATION Per Serving: 284 cal., 5 g fat, 1 g sat. fat, 50 g carb., 12 g protein, 386 mg sodium, 7 g sugar, 6 g fiber.

GRAMMA'S OLD-FASHIONED PANCAKES

Very few breakfast favorites are quite as soul-satisfying and purely filling as well-made pancakes. These wonderful flapjacks are straight out of my Gramma's kitchen, and the flavor is sure to take you back to your happiest childhood memories. This particular recipe, however, will make those memories slimming ones, because the calories are on the low side, as are the fats. A few simple and wholesome ingredients supply all the flavors you could ever want. Rather than indulge in sugar-heavy syrup, try warming a cup of mixed berries over medium heat with a ¼ cup of orange juice—it's an out-of-this-world syrup alternative.

1. In a large bowl, sift together the flour, baking powder, sugar, and salt.

2. Make a well in the center of the dry ingredients and pour in the milk, vanilla extract, butter, and egg. Stir just until mixed and the batter is free of lumps. Let the batter rest for 5 minutes.

3. Coat a large skillet with cooking spray and heat it over medium heat (or heat the skillet over medium heat and add a small amount of melted butter). Pour about ¼ cup of batter into the skillet for each pancake. Cook until golden brown on the underside and then flip. Continue cooking until both sides are brown and serve warm.

NUTRITIONAL INFORMATION Per Serving: 295 cal., 11 g fat, 6 g sat. fat, 39 g carb., 9 g protein, 740 mg sodium, 5 g sugar, 0 g fiber.

SERVES 4

1½ cups all-purpose flour

3 teaspoons baking powder

1 tablespoon granulated sugar

½ teaspoon salt

1¼ cups whole milk

½ teaspoon pure vanilla extract

2 tablespoons unsalted butter, melted, plus more as needed (optional)

1 egg

Cooking spray

Smoked Salmon
and Egg Sandwich

SMOKED SALMON AND EGG SANDWICH

Here's an outstanding reinvention of the classic New York bagel and a schmear. This one cuts back on the fat of the original but captures the true spirit with the indescribably rich flavor of smoked salmon coupled with salty capers and delightfully smooth cream cheese. This version includes egg to round out the meal and add a bit of protein and even more flavor—and English muffins to capture all those other wonderful ingredients.

1. In a small bowl, mash the cream cheese with a rubber spatula until very smooth and spreadable. Add the capers and dill and stir well to combine. Spread about 1 tablespoon of the mixture on the bottom half of each muffin.

2. Coat a large nonstick skillet with cooking spray and heat it over medium heat. Cook the eggs, sunny-side up. Season with salt and pepper to taste, and cook to desired doneness.

3. Set 1 egg on each cream cheese–covered muffin. Divide the salmon among the sandwiches, cover with the muffin tops, and serve.

NUTRITIONAL INFORMATION Per Serving: 272 cal., 9 g fat, 2 g sat. fat, 30 g carb., 20 g protein, 1021 mg sodium, 5 g sugar, 5 g fiber.

SERVES 4

¼ cup fat-free cream cheese, at room temperature

1 teaspoon capers, drained

½ teaspoon dried dill

4 whole-wheat English muffins, split and toasted

Cooking spray

4 large eggs

Salt and freshly ground black pepper, to taste

4 ounces smoked salmon

MEDITERRANEAN BREAKFAST PITA POCKETS

When it's a long time to lunch and you've got a lot to do, you need to pack in highly usable calories to supply long-term energy. Of course, it helps if those calories come in seaside summer flavors that fill you up without slowing you down. A combination of protein-rich eggs and egg whites serves as the base for this savory morning meal. Salty and tart flavors dominate, providing the perfect wake-up call for your taste buds.

SERVES 4

4 large eggs

4 large egg whites

½ teaspoon dried oregano

2 teaspoons extra-virgin olive oil

½ small red onion, thinly sliced

2 tablespoons (about 8) pitted Kalamata olives, chopped

1 ounce crumbled feta cheese

1 vine-ripened tomato, seeded and diced

2 whole-wheat pita sandwich pockets, halved

¼ cup hummus

4 green-leaf lettuce leaves

1. In a medium bowl, whisk together the eggs, egg whites, and oregano.

2. Heat the olive oil in a large nonstick skillet over medium heat. Add the onion and cook until softened, about 4 minutes.

3. Reduce the heat to medium-low. Add the beaten eggs and use a rubber spatula to slowly stir the eggs. Cook until just set but still moist, 2 to 3 minutes. Remove the pan from the heat and scatter the olives, cheese, and tomato over the eggs. Cover the pan and let stand for a couple of minutes to soften the cheese.

4. Open each pita half to create a pocket. Spread a tablespoon of hummus inside each pita and line each pocket with a lettuce leaf. Divide the egg mixture among the pockets and serve warm.

NUTRITIONAL INFORMATION Per Serving: 271 cal., 14 g fat, 4 g sat. fat, 21 g carb., 18 g protein, 438 mg sodium, 3 g sugar, 4 g fiber.

Mediterranean Breakfast
Pita Pockets

INDIVIDUAL MUSHROOM-AND-SWISS QUICHES

Quiche is perhaps the ultimate all-in-one breakfast. These miniature breakfast treats come in a handy package that is low in calories and exceedingly high in luxurious flavors. The quiches are made healthier by combining egg whites with whole eggs and using a small amount of cheese that delivers a large amount of cheesiness.

SERVES 6

Olive oil cooking spray

4 ounces cremini mushrooms, sliced

1 large shallot, minced

Salt and freshly ground black pepper, to taste

4 large eggs

4 large egg whites

¼ teaspoon dried thyme

¼ cup low-fat milk

2 ounces grated Swiss cheese

1. Preheat the oven to 375 degrees F. Spray a 6-portion nonstick jumbo muffin pan with olive oil cooking spray.

2. Coat a large nonstick skillet with cooking spray and heat it over medium-high heat. Add the mushrooms and shallots and season with salt and pepper to taste. Stir frequently until the mushrooms are softened, have released their liquid, and are beginning to brown, 6 to 8 minutes. Divide the mushroom mixture among the cups in the muffin pan.

3. In a large bowl, combine the eggs, egg whites, thyme, milk, and half of the cheese and whisk until thoroughly mixed. Season with salt and pepper.

4. Divide the mixture between the muffin cups and sprinkle the remaining cheese evenly over each portion. Bake until set and the edges are beginning to brown, about 25 minutes. Cool for 5 minutes in the pan before serving.

NUTRITIONAL INFORMATION Per Serving: 115 cal., 7 g fat, 3 g sat. fat, 3 g carb., 9 g protein, 268 mg sodium, 1 g sugar, 0 g fiber.

KALE BAKED EGGS

Kale and eggs? Not the first pairing you'd think of in the morning, but wow, what a combo. The perfect protein source full of all the best oils, combined with the most nutritious green you can buy? Ka-ching. Oh, and a rugged flavor that is rounded out and tamed by some simple additions. Now breakfast just became interesting. And incredibly fun, healthy, and delicious. Thank goodness for odd couples.

1. Preheat the oven to 400 degrees F.

2. Heat the olive oil in an oven-safe, medium nonstick skillet over medium heat. Add the onion and garlic and cook until softened, 3 to 4 minutes. Add the kale, cover, and cook until wilted, about 5 minutes.

3. Remove the lid from the pan and cook until any liquid in the pan has evaporated. Add the nutmeg, salt, and pepper. Remove the pan from the heat.

4. Use a wooden spoon or spatula to make four indentations in the kale, spaced evenly apart in the pan. Crack an egg into each of these "nests." Season with salt and pepper and sprinkle paprika over each egg. Sprinkle with parmesan. Put the pan in the oven.

5. Bake until the eggs are set but the yolks are still runny, 10 to 12 minutes. Remove the pan from the oven and divide the eggs and kale among 4 serving plates. Serve each with a slice of toast.

NUTRITIONAL INFORMATION Per Serving: 287 cal., 13 g fat, 4 g sat. fat, 29 g carb., 16 g protein, 452 mg sodium, 4 g sugar, 4 g fiber.

SERVES 4

1 tablespoon extra-virgin olive oil

1 small yellow onion, chopped

1 clove garlic, minced

1 bunch kale, stems removed and leaves roughly chopped

Pinch freshly grated nutmeg

Dash of salt

Freshly ground black pepper, to taste

4 large eggs

¼ teaspoon sweet paprika

¼ cup grated parmesan

4 slices whole-grain toast

Buckwheat Crêpes with
Cinnamon Honey

BUCKWHEAT CRÊPES WITH CINNAMON HONEY

Crêpes require just a bit of finesse, but the effort is well rewarded. The delicate texture and light sweetness of these crêpes are tempered with an elegant blend of spices that elevate the simple crêpe to something more. Couple that experience with a heavenly honey coating and you have something magical. Airy, delicious, and quick to cook, this breakfast is nothing short of transcendent. You may never settle for pancakes again.

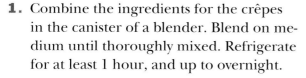

1. Combine the ingredients for the crêpes in the canister of a blender. Blend on medium until thoroughly mixed. Refrigerate for at least 1 hour, and up to overnight.

2. Coat an 8-inch nonstick crêpe pan with cooking spray and heat it over medium heat. Pour about ¼ cup of the batter into the center, and swirl the pan to distribute the batter over the surface of the pan. Cook until the crêpe sets and begins to brown on the underside, about 2 minutes. Run a thin rubber spatula around the edges of the crêpe and carefully flip it. Cook until the underside begins to brown, about 1 minute. Slide the crêpe out onto a plate and cover to keep warm. Repeat with the remaining crêpe batter.

3. In a small pan over medium heat, combine the honey, cinnamon, and nutmeg for the topping. Stir while warming, until combined and heated through. Stir in the lemon zest.

SERVES 4 (ABOUT 16 CRÊPES)

For the crêpes:

1½ cups almond milk

⅔ cup all-purpose flour

⅓ cup buckwheat flour

2 teaspoons packed light brown sugar

2 large eggs

2 tablespoons unsalted butter, melted

Pinch freshly grated nutmeg

Pinch ground dried ginger

Pinch salt

Cooking spray

For the cinnamon honey:

⅓ cup honey

¼ teaspoon ground cinnamon

Pinch grated nutmeg

½ teaspoon lemon zest

Continued

4. Put a crêpe on each of 4 serving plates. Drizzle a little of the honey over each crêpe. Repeat with 2 or 3 more crêpes on each plate, as desired. Serve warm.

NUTRITIONAL INFORMATION Per Serving: 300 cal., 6 g fat, 2 g sat. fat, 54 g carb., 8 g protein, 251 mg sodium, 30 g sugar, 1 g fiber.

CHIA-POMEGRANATE BREAKFAST PUDDING

If you haven't discovered the wonders of chia seeds, you're missing out. This versatile ingredient is a nutrition powerhouse. Chia seeds supply abundant protein, fiber, and essential minerals. They are also rich in antioxidants and beneficial Omega-3 oils. On top of all that, chia seeds absorb moisture like a sponge, making them spectacular additions to a dish like this. Normally the flavor and texture of poppy seeds, fluid-filled chia seeds take on the pleasing, silky mouthfeel of tapioca.

1. In a small bowl, combine the almond milk, vanilla and almond extracts, honey, and chia seeds and whisk to mix. Refrigerate for at least 30 minutes and up to overnight.

2. Fold the yogurt into the milk mixture. Divide among 4 shallow bowls. Top each bowl with the pomegranate seeds and almonds, and serve.

NUTRITIONAL INFORMATION Per Serving: 242 cal., 14 g fat, 1 g sat. fat, 23 g carb., 8 g protein, 90 mg sodium, 9 g sugar, 13 g fiber.

SERVES 4

1½ cups almond milk

½ teaspoon pure vanilla extract

2 drops almond extract

1 teaspoon honey

¼ cup chia seeds

½ cup nonfat vanilla yogurt

⅓ cup pomegranate seeds

¼ cup sliced almonds, toasted

GREEN-CHILI-AND-EGG QUESADILLAS

Sometimes you need something a little bit sharp to wake you up. Chiles, pepper jack, and salsa combine in this dish for a pop-your-eyes-open zip that will get your morning started with a bang. This quesadilla is unlike most other versions because it includes well-scrambled eggs that add a bit of fluffy texture to the dish. Throw the whole thing onto a whole-wheat tortilla and you've got a heart-healthy version of a Mexican favorite.

SERVES 4

Cooking spray

4 large eggs

2 tablespoons low-fat milk

Four 6-inch whole-wheat tortillas

4 ounces low-fat pepper jack cheese, grated

¼ cup green chiles, drained

1. Coat a large nonstick skillet with cooking spray and heat it over medium-low heat.

2. In a small bowl, combine the eggs and milk and whisk until incorporated. Pour the mixture into the pan. Use a rubber spatula to stir the eggs until scrambled but still moist and soft, 3 to 4 minutes.

3. Spread the tortillas out on a work surface and sprinkle one-quarter of the cheese over each. Divide the scrambled eggs among the tortillas and sprinkle 1 tablespoon of the chiles over each. Top with the remaining cheese, fold over, and press down to adhere.

4. Spray the pan again with cooking spray. Cook 1 or 2 quesadillas at a time, depending on how much space you have in the pan. Cook the quesadillas until light golden on the bottom, 3 to 4 minutes. Flip and cook until the tortilla is golden and the cheese is melted, 2 to 3 minutes more.

Continued

Green-Chili-and-
Egg Quesadillas

5. Transfer the cooked quesadillas to a clean plate. Cover to keep warm, and repeat with the remaining quesadillas.

6. Cut each quesadilla into halves and distribute among 4 serving plates.

NUTRITIONAL INFORMATION Per Serving: 294 cal., 17 g fat, 8 g sat. fat, 18 g carb., 16 g protein, 588 mg sodium, 0 g sugar, 3 g fiber.

MELON-BERRY CUPS

Seasonal fruit makes this a stunning breakfast full of lively flavors. It's as beautiful as it is delicious, and can be a stunner for a weekend brunch on a sunny morning. The juicy fruit and perky citrus notes will draw the attention, but there are lots of health reasons to enjoy this dish anytime you can. The cantaloupe delivers a wealth of vitamin A and beta-carotene, and the blueberries are full of antioxidants that boost immune system function and heart health.

1. In a medium bowl, combine the melon, blueberries, mint, and lemon zest, and gently toss.

2. Add ¼ cup of yogurt to each of 4 wide glasses or small bowls. Divide the melon mixture among the glasses and sprinkle the sunflower seeds on top. Serve immediately or refrigerate for up to 1 hour.

NUTRITIONAL INFORMATION Per Serving: 130 cal., 5 g fat, 0 g sat. fat, 18 g carb., 6 g protein, 57 mg sodium, 14 g sugar, 3 g fiber.

SERVES 4

2 cups cubed cantaloupe (or substitute watermelon, honeydew, or a combination)

1 cup blueberries

4 sprigs fresh mint, leaves stripped and finely chopped

Zest of ½ lemon

1 cup nonfat vanilla yogurt

¼ cup roasted, unsalted sunflower seeds

Apple-Walnut Grits

APPLE-WALNUT GRITS

Oatmeal has met its match. This scrumptious day-starter boasts a creaminess that sets it apart from other breakfast options, and the flavor is complex, deep, and rich. Apple and walnut flavors go naturally with grits and, along with the cinnamon in this dish, create a truly satisfying first meal of the day. And though true Southerners may think it a scandal to use quick-cooking grits, they ensure a simple meal that you can throw together in a hurry.

1. In a medium saucepan over medium heat, combine the apple juice, almond milk, grits, and cinnamon. Whisk to combine and bring to a simmer while stirring.

2. Reduce the heat to medium-low and cook, stirring often, until thickened.

3. Divide the grits among 4 bowls and top each with the walnuts and apple.

NUTRITIONAL INFORMATION Per Serving: 181 cal., 13 g fat, 1 g sat. fat, 20 g carb., 7 g protein, 115 mg sodium, 11 g sugar, 2 g fiber.

SERVES 4

1 cup apple juice, not from concentrate

1½ cups vanilla light almond milk

½ cup quick-cooking grits

½ teaspoon ground cinnamon

¼ cup toasted walnuts, chopped

1 red apple, cored and diced

CHOCOLATE WHOLE-GRAIN WAFFLES
WITH STRAWBERRY SYRUP

Chocolate and strawberries spell decadence for breakfast. The flavors are perfect partners that delight the tongue and are a wonderful taste sensation to get any day off to a great start. As fun and indulgent as those flavors might be, all the ingredients in these waffles are wholesome and healthy, with a minimum of sugar and calories. This is truly a guilt-free treat that brings a smile to the morning meal.

SERVES 4

½ cup whole-grain waffle mix

¼ cup almond milk (or substitute soy milk)

¼ cup unsweetened cocoa powder

1 tablespoon honey

2 cups chopped fresh strawberries (or substitute frozen)

½ cup apple juice, not from concentrate

1. In a large bowl, prepare the waffle mix according to the package instructions. Add the almond milk, cocoa powder, and honey and mix well. Preheat a waffle iron and cook the waffles according to the manufacturer's instructions.

2. While the waffles are cooking, combine the strawberries, apple juice, and ½ cup water in a large saucepan over medium heat. Bring to a boil and then reduce the heat to a simmer. Cook for 10 minutes.

3. Strain the syrup through a fine mesh strainer set over a pitcher. Discard the solids.

4. Serve the waffles warm with the strawberry syrup drizzled over the top.

NUTRITIONAL INFORMATION Per Serving: 104 cal., 1 g fat, 1 g sat. fat, 23 g carb., 4 g protein, 178 mg sodium, 9 g sugar, 4 g fiber.

Chocolate Whole-Grain
Waffles

Broiled
Almond-Banana Toast

BROILED ALMOND-BANANA TOAST

If you've ever enjoyed simple cinnamon toast, this creation takes the idea to the next level. Almond butter supplies a smooth, luscious element that counterbalances the crunch of the toast. The butter also complements the cinnamon perfectly and works like a charm with the bananas as well. This is a great on-the-go breakfast for anyone in a rush, one that will give you all the energy you need to conquer the morning.

1. Preheat the broiler and position a rack 6 to 8 inches from the heat source.

2. Place the bread slices on a baking sheet. Spread about 1½ tablespoons of the almond butter on each slice, covering the bread completely. Arrange the banana slices on top of each slice in a single layer.

3. In a small bowl, combine the sugar, cinnamon, and ginger and stir to mix. Sprinkle the sugar evenly over the top of the banana slices.

4. Broil the slices, watching carefully. Remove them when the sugar caramelizes on top of the bananas, 1 to 2 minutes. Cool briefly before serving.

NUTRITIONAL INFORMATION Per Serving: 282 cal., 29 g fat, 3 g sat. fat, 103 g carb., 23 g protein, 328 mg sodium, 50 g sugar, 16 g fiber.

SERVES 4

4 slices whole-grain bread, toasted

⅓ cup natural almond butter

2 bananas, thinly sliced

2 tablespoons sugar

¼ teaspoon ground cinnamon

Pinch ground dried ginger

MIDDAY RECIPES

3

The Power to Get Through

Green Bean and Artichoke Stir-fry

Zucchini, Corn, and Pepper Hash

Herb-Roasted Parsnips and Carrots

Nutty Brown Rice Pilaf

Asparagus with Lemony Breadcrumbs

Steamed Sesame Bok Choy

Chile-Lime Sweet Potatoes

Cauliflower Steaks with Tomato Relish

Cucumber Gazpacho

Spicy Carrot and Celery Root Soup

Dilled Tuna and Chickpea Salad Sandwiches

Pan-Seared Citrus Chicken

Turkey, Apple, and Cheddar Panini

Pork Tenderloin Sandwich with Artichoke Spread

Energizing Avocado-Chicken Salad

Orzo Salad with Shrimp, Cucumbers, and Feta

Greens and Grains Salad

Tomato and Mozzarella Salad with Smoked Paprika Vinaigrette

Roasted Beets with Arugula, Pistachios, and Lemon-Scented Ricotta

Grapefruit and Hearts of Palm Salad with Honey-Lime Vinaigrette

Baby Spinach Salad with Crispy Shallots and Smoked Gouda

Uncle Johnny's Black-Eyed Pea Salad

Meat-packing Peppers

Chickpea and Celery Salad with Lemon-Parmesan Dressing

Quinoa with Dandelion Greens, Apples, and Pecans

Butter Lettuce with Oranges, Olives, and Tarragon Vinaigrette

Watercress and Endive with Avocado, Melon, and Toasted Hazelnuts

Protein-Packed Turkey Burger

The concept of smaller meals is nothing new, but on a SHRED plan it's particularly important. Trying to get in four small to moderate meals a day means that each meal needs to be substantial enough to satisfy but not so substantial that you're consuming too many calories. In the SHRED lifestyle, meals 3 and 4 typically occur between 11 A.M. and 4 P.M. That's why I call them midday meals. Unlike the great tradition of one huge meal in the middle of the day, those calories are broken up and spread over two meals. These meals are critical because they power us through what is often the busiest part of the day, when our energy needs can be at their greatest. This is not a time to skip meals; rather, it is a time to refuel and to do so with predicted regularity as you train your body to expect its nourishment on a reliable schedule.

The recipes in this section have different calorie counts. The amount of calories you are trying to consume for that meal will dictate which recipes you choose. If one recipe has too many calories and you really want to have it, simply make calorie-reducing substitutions that will bring the calorie count within the guidelines that you desire. For example, if you don't want to add low-fat milk that's called for in a recipe but would rather have light almond milk, that substitution would be completely fine. But substituting a cup of whole milk for low-fat milk would not be advised because of the increase in calories.

These meals need to power you through the rest of your day, so choose them wisely. Fiber is always a great op-tion because it will fill you up on fewer calories. Many of the recipes here can be complemented with a small garden salad, filling you up without adding many calories to the main dish. Remember that these midday meals should be spaced about 3 hours apart. If you get hungry between the meals, a 150-calorie or less snack can get keep you going.

Portion control is important, so be careful not to overdo it. It's in the middle of the day that we tend to be overly generous with the quantity of ingredients and servings. If you're preparing something that has multiple servings and you'll be the only person eating, go ahead and prepare the entire recipe, but make sure that you only eat the designated single serving. Pack up and store the remainder to eat it at a different time.

You will find plenty of soups in this section, and that is not by accident. Soups can fill you up on fewer calories, and SHRED soups are chock-full of vitamins, fiber, minerals, and other nutrients. Another advantage of soups is their convenience. You can prepare them, package them, and take them with you to work an event or on a trip. Soups can be a dieter's best friend, especially when you take the time to prepare them for yourself so that you know the ingredients, calorie counts, and serving size. Take advantage of these tasty recipes, and whenever possible choose as many fresh ingredients as you can to make them.

One trick you might try before each midday meal is to consume an 8-ounce glass of water. This will help you consume less food and thus fewer calories. Another tip with these meals is to try to consume the healthier items first (veggies). While room for more calories diminishes, you'll leave more of the unhealthier items on the plate. The midday recipes are here for you to sample, have fun, feel satisfied, and enjoy.

ROASTED RED PEPPER SOUP

The deep flavor of roasted red peppers is an ideal in soup because the flavor seems filling without the soup actually being heavy. The secret in this version is a dose of sweet paprika, which reinforces the smoky flavor of the peppers and gives the soup more depth. Like many of the soups following this section, this one can be frozen in individual servings for quick meals later in the week.

1. Heat the olive oil in a large saucepan over medium-high heat. Add the onion and garlic and cook until softened but not browned, about 4 minutes. Add the paprika and cook for about 1 minute.

2. Add the red peppers and chicken stock and bring to a boil. Reduce the heat to medium-low, cover, and simmer for about 10 minutes.

3. Working in batches, purée the soup in the blender and return it to the saucepan. Keep warm until ready to serve.

4. Ladle the soup into warm bowls; top with a small dollop of yogurt; and garnish with basil, if using.

NUTRITIONAL INFORMATION Per Serving: 79 cal., 4 g fat, 1 g sat. fat, 4 g carb., 3 g protein, 460 mg sodium, 1 g sugar, 4 g fiber.

SERVES 4 (MAKES ABOUT 6 CUPS)

1 tablespoon extra-virgin olive oil

1 yellow onion, chopped

1 clove garlic, smashed

½ teaspoon sweet paprika

One 12-ounce jar roasted red peppers, drained and coarsely chopped

1 quart low-sodium chicken stock (or substitute vegetable broth)

2 tablespoons nonfat Greek yogurt

Sliced fresh basil, for optional garnish

Roasted Red
Pepper Soup

HEART-LOVING CHICKEN TERIYAKI

The next time you have a hankering for a taste of Asia, don't grab that takeout menu—instead, pick up some fresh chicken thighs, a handy bag of stir-fry vegetables, and make your own healthy fast food. This dish is low in cholesterol and high in essential healthy fats—like the monounsaturated fatty acids in olive oil and the beneficial oils in chicken thighs. All that healthiness aside, this dish delivers big flavor. Rather than the traditional grilling, the chicken here is pan-cooked, preserving moisture and tenderness and speeding up the process. A marinade that doubles as a sauce makes the meal even easier and quicker.

1. In a nonreactive medium bowl, combine the pineapple juice, 2 tablespoons olive oil, the sesame oil, soy sauce, brown sugar, garlic powder, pepper, and ginger. Whisk until the marinade is completely mixed.

2. Add the chicken to the bowl, cover and refrigerate for at least 30 minutes and up to 2 hours.

3. Heat the remaining olive oil in large nonstick saucepan over medium heat. Reserving the marinade, sauté the chicken until it browns slightly.

4. Add the marinade to the pan and increase the heat to high. Boil for 1 minute, and then reduce the heat to a simmer. Add the vegetables, cover, and cook for 7 minutes.

SERVES 4

½ cup pineapple juice

4 tablespoons extra-virgin olive oil

Dash of sesame oil

¼ cup low-sodium soy sauce

2 tablespoons light brown sugar

½ teaspoon garlic powder

¼ teaspoon freshly ground black pepper

2 teaspoons ground dried ginger

1½ pounds chicken thighs, cut into bite-sized pieces

One 16-ounce bag frozen stir-fry vegetables

Continued

5. Remove the chicken from the pan with tongs and set aside. Increase the heat to high and boil the sauce until it thickens to syrup consistency. Return the chicken to the pan, stir to coat, and serve.

NUTRITIONAL INFORMATION Per Serving: 623 cal., 45 g fat, 11 g sat. fat, 19 g carb., 28 g protein, 716 mg sodium, 9 g sugar, 3 g fiber.

WHOLE-WHEAT PASTA WITH CHERRY TOMATOES AND BASIL

This is the simplest pasta preparation that you can make when you have very few ingredients on hand. Toss in tuna or grilled chicken strips if you need a protein fix. The leftovers hold well for pasta salad the next day, with more added veggies or pitted olives.

1. Liberally salt a stockpot full of water and bring to a boil over medium-high heat.

2. Add the pasta and cook according to package instructions or until al dente, about 8 minutes.

3. When the pasta is almost finished cooking, remove 2 tablespoons of the cooking water and whisk together with the olive oil.

4. Drain the pasta in a colander, shaking it to remove excess cooking water.

5. Remove the pasta to a serving bowl and toss immediately with the olive oil mixture, the tomatoes, and the basil.

6. Season with salt and pepper to taste before serving.

NUTRITIONAL INFORMATION Per Serving: 238 cal., 4 g fat, 0 g sat. fat, 45 g carb., 6 g protein, 161 mg sodium, 2 g sugar, 7 g fiber.

SERVES 8

1 pound whole-wheat pasta shells (DeLallo if available, okay to substitute regular pasta)

1 tablespoon olive oil

1 pint cherry tomatoes, halved

1 cup basil leaves, thinly sliced

Salt and pepper, to taste

Mmmeat Loaf
Muffins

MMMEAT LOAF MUFFINS

Muffins aren't just for dessert anymore. At least not when you redefine them as a savory treat filled with lean, succulent beef. (You can even "frost" the muffins with some nonfat sour cream!) They are also perfect as snacks, a quick lunch, or part of a larger meal. You can make them ahead of time and freeze them prior to cooking. Just pull them out, pop them in the oven, and in no time flat you have an amusing protein-rich dish.

1. Preheat the oven to 375 degrees F. Spray a 12-cup muffin tin with oil.

2. In a small bowl, whisk together the ketchup, brown sugar, and mustard. Set aside.

3. In a large bowl, break apart the beef with your fingers. Add the tomatoes, oats, Worcestershire sauce, eggs, onion, and bell pepper. Season with salt and pepper and, using your hands, mix the ingredients. Do not overwork.

4. Divide the mixture among the muffin cups. Spread 2 teaspoons of the sauce on each.

5. Bake until an instant-read thermometer inserted in center of a loaf reads 160 degrees F, 25 to 30 minutes. Let cool in the muffin pan on a rack for 10 minutes before removing and serving.

NUTRITIONAL INFORMATION Per Serving: 194 cal., 13 g fat, 4 g sat. fat, 9 g carb., 12 g protein, 386 mg sodium, 5 g sugar, 1 g fiber.

SERVES 12

Cooking spray

For the sauce:

⅔ cup ketchup

1 tablespoon brown sugar

1 tablespoon yellow mustard

For the muffins:

1½ pounds ground beef

One 8-ounce can diced tomatoes

½ cup quick-cooking oats

1 tablespoon Worcestershire sauce

2 large eggs, lightly beaten

1 medium onion, minced

½ cup diced bell pepper

½ teaspoon salt

½ teaspoon pepper

SQUASH SOUP WITH FARRO AND ALMONDS

A favorite in Italy, the full-bodied grain farro is growing in popularity as more and more people discover its robust qualities. (However, anyone with gluten sensitivity or celiac disease should avoid farro.) The chewy texture of the grain perfectly contrasts the silkiness of squash. Add in almonds and a few basic seasonings and you've got a heart-smart, rich, and sweet soup that provides abundant fiber and A, C, and B vitamins.

**SERVES 4 TO 6
(MAKES ABOUT 8 CUPS)**

1 tablespoon extra-virgin olive oil

2 large shallots, chopped

2 cloves garlic, smashed

1 small butternut squash (about 2 pounds), peeled, seeded, and coarsely chopped

1 bay leaf

⅛ teaspoon freshly grated nutmeg

Pinch cayenne pepper

1 quart low-sodium chicken stock (or substitute vegetable broth)

Salt and pepper, to taste

½ cup farro, cooked according to package instructions

¼ cup sliced almonds, toasted

1. Heat the olive oil in a large saucepan over medium-high heat. Add the shallots and garlic and cook until softened but not browned, about 4 minutes. Add the squash, bay leaf, nutmeg, cayenne, and chicken stock. Season lightly with salt and pepper and bring the soup to a boil.

2. Reduce the heat to medium-low, cover, and simmer until the squash is completely soft and falling apart, about 20 minutes. Remove the bay leaf.

3. Working in small batches, purée the soup in a blender until smooth and return it to the saucepan. If the soup is too thick, add a little more chicken stock until the desired consistency is reached.

4. Season with salt and pepper to taste. Divide the cooked farro among soup bowls and ladle the warm soup over the grain. Garnish with almonds and serve.

NUTRITIONAL INFORMATION Per Serving: 205 cal., 8 g fat, 1 g sat. fat, 30 g carb., 6 g protein, 275 mg sodium, 7 g sugar, 8 g fiber.

AUNTIE LYNN'S SOUTHERN CABBAGE

Cabbage is a little-known superstar in the world of healthy foods. It offers amazing health benefits, thanks to compounds called glucosinolates. This cruciferous vegetable is rich in these compounds, which are closely linked to cancer prevention. Cabbage also boasts anti-inflammatory agents and gastrointestinal benefits (it's been shown to aid in the healing of peptic ulcers!). And best of all, this brassica is easy to cook and include on the dinner table. This simple side dish goes with meat, fish, and chicken equally well and can even stand in as a quick and delicious meal-in-one for those vegetarians or pure cabbage lovers at your table. When my Aunt Lynn makes this dish, the entire family is sitting at the table, forks in hand, ready to dig in!

1. In a large pot over high heat, heat the olive oil until hot.

2. Add the cabbage, onion powder, red pepper flakes, salt, and pepper. Stir to thoroughly mix the ingredients and then reduce the heat to medium.

3. Cover and cook until cabbage is fork-tender, or done to your preference.

NUTRITIONAL INFORMATION Per Serving: 228 cal., 18 g fat, 3 g sat. fat, 16 g carb., 4 g protein, 138 mg sodium, 8 g sugar, 6 g fiber.

SERVES 4

⅓ cup extra-virgin olive oil

1 large head cabbage, cut into eight wedges, cleaned

2 tablespoons onion powder

Pinch crushed red pepper flakes

Pinch sea salt

Pinch freshly ground black pepper

HEAVENLY CHEESEBURGER

A great cheeseburger is a simple thing, but hard to perfect. The problem with many burgers is that they dry out because the meat is too lean. This juicy handheld feast beats that problem by adding plenty of wet ingredients into the mix and by using ground sirloin rather than the more common ground chuck. Not only is the flavor better in sirloin but it also delivers a big burst of protein. Do yourself a favor and have your sirloin ground fresh by a butcher. Use the meat as soon as you get home, or freeze it right away to preserve the flavor and moisture.

SERVES 4

1 pound ground sirloin

¼ teaspoon seasoning salt

1 teaspoon Worcestershire sauce

1 teaspoon barbecue sauce

1 tablespoon unsalted butter

4 slices reduced-sodium American cheese

4 light wheat hamburger rolls

4 slices tomato

4 leaves lettuce

1. In a large bowl, combine the meat with the seasoning salt and Worcestershire sauce. Use your hands to mix the ingredients. Add the barbecue sauce and mix it in.

2. Divide the mixture into four equal patties and flatten to ½-inch thick.

3. In a large skillet over medium heat, melt the butter. Brown the patties on both sides. When they are almost done, lay a slice of cheese on top of each patty.

4. Serve each burger on a bun with a slice of tomato and a lettuce leaf.

NUTRITIONAL INFORMATION Per Serving: 360 cal., 16 g fat, 8 g sat. fat, 21 g carb., 31 g protein, 379 mg sodium, 4 g sugar, 5 g fiber.

SERIOUSLY SIMPLE CHICKEN SALAD

Making the perfect chicken salad doesn't have to mean slaving away in the kitchen for hours. This version could easily come right off the menu of a great deli, but it takes only minutes to prepare—all thanks to the blender. That makes it a super option for weeknights when you're pressed for time, need to get dinner on the table, and don't have much in the way of culinary inspiration. The addition of avocado and cilantro gives the salad a slightly south-of-the-border flair and pleasingly complex mouthfeel. You'll be amazed at how little time and effort it takes to bring such fresh and fun flavors to life.

1. Combine chicken, avocado, bell pepper, vinaigrette, cilantro and scallions in the canister of a blender. Pulse until the texture is coarse and the mixture is well blended.

2. Divide the salad between the four buns, top with a slice of tomato, and serve.

NUTRITIONAL INFORMATION Per Serving: 291 cal., 19 g fat, 2 g sat. fat, 31 g carb., 28 g protein, 475 mg sodium, 10 g sugar, 4 g fiber.

SERVES 4

2 cups chopped, cooked, skinless, boneless chicken breast

¼ avocado, chopped

½ red bell pepper, cleaned and chopped

½ cup low-fat herb vinaigrette

¼ cup chopped fresh cilantro

2 scallions, cleaned, trimmed, and cut in half

4 whole-wheat buns

4 slices tomato

ROASTED CAULIFLOWER CURRY SOUP

Cauliflower can tend toward blandness but not when you roast it. Roasting this white vegetable adds a delicate smokiness and brings out the natural, if understated, sweetness. This soup combines two classic flavors by mixing the bite of curry with the smoky goodness of the roasted cauliflower. That partnership is accented with a few spices and nothing more and comes out intriguing without being overwhelming. It's pleasant on the tongue and wholesome for the body and soul.

SERVES 4 (MAKES ABOUT 6 CUPS)

1 head cauliflower (2 to 3 pounds), cut into small florets

2 tablespoons extra-virgin olive oil

Salt and pepper, to taste

1 small white onion, chopped

2 cloves garlic, chopped

1 small bay leaf

1 teaspoon mild curry powder, plus more as needed

Pinch cayenne pepper

1 quart vegetable broth

1. Preheat the oven to 450 degrees F. Line a baking sheet with parchment paper.

2. Spread the cauliflower in an even layer on the baking sheet. Drizzle 1 tablespoon of the olive oil over the cauliflower and toss it well to coat.

3. Dust the cauliflower with salt and pepper, and roast, tossing occasionally with a spatula until golden brown, for about 20 minutes. Remove from the oven and reserve about 1 cup of the smallest florets.

4. While the cauliflower roasts, heat the remaining 1 tablespoon of the olive oil in a large saucepan over medium heat. Add the onion, garlic, bay leaf, curry, and cayenne and cook slowly until very soft, about 10 minutes.

5. Add the roasted cauliflower to the pan along with the vegetable broth. Bring the mixture to a boil and cover. Cook until the cauliflower is completely tender, about 10 minutes. Remove the bay leaf.

6. Working in batches, purée the soup in a blender and return it to the saucepan. Season with additional salt, pepper, and curry to taste

7. Ladle the warm soup into bowls and scatter the reserved roasted cauliflower florets over the top before serving.

NUTRITIONAL INFORMATION Per Serving: 138 cal., 7 g fat, g sat. 1 fat, 14 g carb., 3 g protein, 335 mg sodium, 6 g sugar, 5 g fiber.

ZESTY LEMON-HERB CHICKEN

The best way to do justice to the culinary canvas that is chicken breast meat is to create an alluring blend of aromatic flavors that simply sparkle on the tongue. Replacing the more traditional bath of beaten eggs or olive oil, these cutlets are prepared with a bright canola–lemon juice bath that marries perfectly with the Mediterranean herbs in the breading. The flavors are so complete that the cutlets need nothing more than a garnish of lemon wedges, though they can also be ideal partners for a small helping of spaghetti or orecchiette in a simple tomato sauce.

SERVES 4

Cooking spray

½ cup breadcrumbs

1 teaspoon lemon pepper

1 tablespoon rosemary leaves

¼ teaspoon garlic powder

¼ teaspoon salt

4 tablespoons lemon juice

2 tablespoons canola oil

Four 6-ounce skinless, boneless chicken breasts

1. Preheat the oven to 400 degrees F. Coat a baking sheet with cooking spray.

2. Combine the breadcrumbs, lemon pepper, rosemary, garlic powder, and salt in a 1-gallon resealable plastic bag.

3. In a shallow bowl, combine the lemon juice and canola oil. Whisk to incorporate. Dip each chicken breast into the mixture and let any excess drip into the bowl.

4. Transfer the chicken breasts to the dry mix in the plastic bag, seal, and shake well to coat.

5. Transfer to the baking sheet and bake for 20 to 25 minutes, or until the chicken is cooked through.

NUTRITIONAL INFORMATION Per Serving: 257 cal., 12 g fat, 2 g sat. fat, 11 g carb., 27 g protein, 264 mg sodium, 1 g sugar, 0 g fiber.

SMOKY LENTIL SOUP

Think lentils are too plain to make a vibrant soup? Think again. These legumes set the stage for intriguing flavor in a soup that combines the meaty essence of turkey bacon along with enchanting smoked paprika and the sharp, fresh edge of cilantro. You'll cook it for the flavor, but you'll be happy you did so for the outstanding health benefits. Low in fat and high in protein, this is one bowl-filler that won't slow you down or add to your waistline.

1. In a medium saucepan over medium heat, combine the bacon and canola oil. Cook, stirring, until crisp. Add the garlic and cook until softened, 2 to 3 minutes. Add the ginger, tomato, and paprika and cook until the tomato begins to break down, 2 to 3 minutes.

2. Add the lentils, cilantro stems, and vegetable broth. Bring to a boil and then reduce the heat to medium-low.

3. Cover and cook until the lentils are breaking down and soup is thick, about 20 minutes.

4. Ladle the soup into individual bowls and garnish with a dollop of the yogurt and a sprinkling of chopped cilantro.

NUTRITIONAL INFORMATION Per Serving: 286 cal., 4 g fat, 0 g sat. fat, 47 g carb., 19 g protein, 387 mg sodium, 9 g sugar, 2 g fiber.

**SERVES 4
(MAKES ABOUT 8 CUPS)**

3 slices turkey bacon, chopped

1 teaspoon canola oil

2 cloves garlic, minced

1 teaspoon grated fresh, peeled ginger

1 large tomato, seeded and diced

½ teaspoon smoked paprika

2 cups lentils, picked over and rinsed

4 cilantro stems, finely chopped, plus chopped leaves for garnish

7 cups low-sodium vegetable broth

¼ cup nonfat Greek yogurt (or substitute nonfat sour cream)

Aunt Lynn's
Slammin' Yams

AUNTIE LYNN'S SLAMMIN' YAMS

Starchy though they may be, the carbohydrates in yams are complex enough to keep the tuber on the low end of the glycemic index—even when they are way high on the flavor index. Yams boast high levels of antioxidants and vitamin A, as well as excellent levels of other vitamins. The smooth texture and full body serve as a foundation for the complex sweet flavors in this dish, making it a heck of a dessert or a special-occasion side dish. Just the smell wafting from the kitchen when my Aunt Lynn cooks this makes my mouth water. This healthy twist on a Southern dish is an all-time favorite.

1. Preheat the oven to 350 degrees F.

2. Peel the yams and trim the ends. Slice lengthwise into ¼-inch slices. Wash in cold water, and then spread the slices out evenly in a medium baking dish.

3. Sprinkle the white and brown sugars evenly over the yams. Sprinkle the nutmeg, cinnamon, vanilla extract, and agave nectar evenly over the yams, in that order.

4. Slice the butter into ¼-inch pats, and top the yams with the butter. Cover the baking dish with aluminum foil.

5. Bake until the yams are tender, about 30 minutes. Periodically check the yams as they bake, and spoon the melted ingredients over the yams.

NUTRITIONAL INFORMATION Per Serving: 288 cal., 7 g fat, 5 g sat. fat, 27 g carb., 1 g protein, 23 mg sodium, 37 g sugar, 7 g fiber.

SERVES 4

2 medium yams

¼ cup granulated sugar

¼ cup dark brown sugar

2 tablespoons ground nutmeg

4 tablespoons ground cinnamon

3 tablespoons pure vanilla extract

2 tablespoons agave nectar

½ stick unsalted butter, chilled

TOMATO AND WHITE BEAN SOUP

As wonderful as tomato soup is, it's even more wonderful when you add the silky smoothness and faint nuttiness of white beans. These two go together perfectly, the acidity of the tomatoes cutting through the richness of the beans. This recipe delivers a good dose of lycopene, an anti-oxidant proven to help fight cancer.

SERVES 4 (MAKES ABOUT 6 CUPS)

1 tablespoon extra-virgin olive oil

1 yellow onion, chopped

2 cloves garlic, minced

1 teaspoon tomato paste

1 large sprig fresh thyme

1 small bay leaf

Freshly ground black pepper, to taste

One 15-ounce can diced tomatoes, with liquid

One 15-ounce can white beans (cannellini or navy), drained

1 quart low-sodium chicken stock (or substitute low-sodium vegetable broth)

1. Heat the olive oil in a large saucepan over medium-high heat. Add the onion and garlic and cook until softened, about 4 minutes. Add the tomato paste and cook, stirring, until the paste begins to caramelize, 2 to 3 minutes.

2. Add the thyme, bay leaf, and pepper. Add the tomatoes and liquid and bring the mixture to a boil. Cook until most of the liquid evaporates, about 5 minutes.

3. Add the beans and chicken stock and cook until the beans begin to break down, about 10 minutes.

4. Remove the bay leaf and thyme sprig. Carefully transfer about 1 cup of the soup to a food processor, purée, and return the mixture to the saucepan (or use a hand-held immersion mixer to purée about one-quarter of the soup in the saucepan, until it has thickened). Season with pepper as necessary and serve warm.

NUTRITIONAL INFORMATION Per Serving: 170 cal., 4 g fat, 1 g sat. fat, 23 g carb., 6 g protein, 467 mg sodium, 5 g sugar, 5 g fiber.

Tomato and White
Bean Soup

Soba Noodles in
Mushroom Broth

SOBA NOODLES IN MUSHROOM BROTH

This dish comes from Japan, where soba noodles reign supreme. If you've never had this spaghetti alternative, you're in for a treat. The flat noodles are made from buckwheat flour, which gives soba its signature strong nutty flavor. You can find gluten-free soba noodles if you have a gluten sensitivity, but either way, the noodle is perfect in a heady soup that includes a touch of ginger, shiitake mushrooms, and delicious baby bok choy.

1. Heat the vegetable broth and soy sauce in a medium saucepan over medium heat until very hot. Turn off the heat, add the dried mushrooms, cover, and let stand for about 10 minutes.

2. With a slotted spoon, remove the dried mushrooms and finely chop them. Carefully pour the broth into another saucepan, leaving any sediment from the mushrooms behind. Add the chopped dried mushrooms to the liquid and keep the broth warm over low heat.

3. Heat the olive oil in a large skillet over medium-high heat. Add the sliced fresh mushrooms and season with salt and pepper to taste. Cook, stirring, until they release their moisture and begin to brown, about 10 minutes.

4. Add the garlic and ginger and cook until softened, 3 to 4 minutes. Transfer the mushroom mixture to the warm broth and bring the liquid to a simmer.

SERVES 4

1 quart vegetable broth

1 teaspoon low-sodium soy sauce

¼ cup dried shiitake mushrooms

1 tablespoon extra-virgin olive oil

8 ounces fresh shiitake mushrooms, sliced

Salt and freshly ground black pepper, to taste

2 cloves garlic, chopped

1 teaspoon grated fresh, peeled ginger

4 heads baby bok choy, chopped

Continued

8 ounces soba noodles, cooked according to package instructions and rinsed in cold water

4 scallions, sliced

5. Add the bok choy to the simmering broth and cook until bright green but still crisp and tender, 2 to 3 minutes. Add the soba noodles to the pan and cook just until the liquid returns to a simmer and the noodles are hot.

6. Divide the noodles and broth among 4 large, shallow bowls. Scatter the scallions over the broth and serve with chopsticks.

NUTRITIONAL INFORMATION Per Serving: 110 cal., 4 g fat, 1 g sat. fat, 17 g carb., 5 g protein, 275 mg sodium, 2 g sugar, 4 g fiber.

ROASTED FENNEL WITH LEMON

Fennel's licorice tones become more subdued and sophisticated when roasted, making an alluring side dish that may just draw attention away from the main course. Roasting the fennel with lemon adds the slightest bite to the root vegetable, elevating the dish and enhancing the role that the simple spices play. You don't need anything else to make this a winner, and it's an elegant addition to any meal and any protein—from meatloaf to crown roast to a plate of salmon steaks. The best part is that you won't break a sweat getting it on the table—the oven does most of the work.

1. Preheat the oven to 400 degrees F.

2. Trim the stalks and fronds off the fennel bulbs. Reserve the fronds and cut the stalks into 1-inch pieces. Spread the pieces on a baking sheet.

3. Stand a trimmed bulb upright on a cutting board and slice it in half through the core. Place each half cut-side down on the board and slice the halves into ½-inch-thick wedges through the core. Repeat with the other bulb. Spread the fennel slices on the baking sheet.

4. Add the lemon slices and garlic cloves to the fennel. Drizzle the olive oil evenly over the vegetables. Toss to coat well. Season with the celery salt, salt, and pepper to taste.

5. Roast the fennel, turning once or twice, until very soft and the edges begin to turn golden brown (about 40 minutes).

SERVES 4

2 large bulbs fennel

1 lemon, very thinly sliced, seeds removed

3 cloves garlic, peeled and smashed

3 tablespoons extra-virgin olive oil

¼ teaspoon celery salt

Salt and freshly ground black pepper, to taste

Continued

6. Let cool briefly on the pan. Chop the reserved fronds, scatter them over the roasted fennel, and toss. Transfer the mixture to a serving bowl and serve warm.

NUTRITIONAL INFORMATION Per Serving: 150 cal., 11 g fat, 2 g sat. fat, 12 g carb., 2 g protein, 224 mg sodium, 0 g sugar, 1 g fiber.

BROCCOLI AND TOASTED GARLIC SOUP

Broccoli's true nature comes out in a soup, where the sturdy vegetable is broken down until just nutrients and demure flavor remain. Toasted garlic is broccoli's best friend; the assertive deep richness of the garlic is the ideal counterpoint to the broccoli's simple, earthy, and fresh taste. Blend these in a soup and you create a dish that is greater than the sum of its simple parts—not to mention downright easy to make.

1. Heat the olive oil in a large saucepan over medium-low heat. Add the garlic and cook just until the slices turn very light golden brown. Do not overcook or the garlic will be bitter. Transfer the garlic to a paper towel-lined plate to drain.

2. Increase the heat to medium-high and add the onion and celery to the pan. Cook until the onion is softened, about 5 minutes. Add the potato and chicken stock and bring the mixture to a boil. Cover, reduce to simmer, and cook for 10 minutes.

3. Add the broccoli to the pan and cover. Cook until the broccoli is bright green and very soft, 6 to 8 minutes. Remove the soup from the heat and stir in the parsley leaves.

4. Working in small batches, purée the soup in a blender or with a handheld immersion blender, and return it to the pan. If the soup is too thick, thin with a little chicken stock. Season with pepper to taste.

SERVES 4 (MAKES ABOUT 8 CUPS)

1 tablespoon extra-virgin olive oil

3 large cloves garlic, very thinly sliced

1 small white onion, chopped

2 stalks celery, sliced

1 small russet potato, peeled and diced

1 quart low-sodium chicken stock (or substitute low-sodium vegetable broth)

1 pound fresh broccoli florets, chopped

¼ cup fresh, flat-leaf parsley leaves, plus more chopped for garnish

Continued

5. Ladle the warm soup into bowls and garnish with toasted garlic slices and chopped parsley.

NUTRITIONAL INFORMATION Per Serving: 112 cal., 4 g fat, 1 g sat. fat, 18 g carb., 3 g protein, 177 mg sodium, 2 g sugar, 2 g fiber.

BARLEY WITH ROASTED MUSHROOMS

Dig into a bowl of this filling, richly full-flavored delight and you'll be shocked to learn it's a low-cal dinner. Barley mimics the lush, creamy mouth-feel of cooked pasta in an easy to digest small-ball form. But unlike semolina pastas, this grain provides a goodly amount of essential nutrients and micronutrients. More than that, it's an excellent source of fiber, helping to lower cholesterol and maintain intestinal health. Ultimately, most people to turn to barley for the wonderful way it blends with other earthy ingredients.

1. Preheat the oven to 400 degrees F.

2. Scatter the mushrooms on a baking sheet. Drizzle with the olive oil and toss to coat. Season with salt and pepper.

3. Roast the mushrooms, turning several times with a spatula, until golden brown and beginning to crisp, 35 to 40 minutes.

4. Coat a large skillet with olive oil cooking spray and heat it over medium-high heat.

5. Add the onion, garlic, and thyme. Stir until softened, about 5 minutes. Add the roasted mushrooms and barley. Stir for about 2 minutes.

6. Slowly add the chicken stock, stirring until the liquid has been absorbed. Stir in the parmesan until creamy. Season with additional salt and pepper to taste. Serve warm.

NUTRITIONAL INFORMATION Per Serving: 186 cal., 8 g fat, 2 g sat. fat, 24 g carb., 4 g protein, 212 mg sodium, 2 g sugar, 4 g fiber.

SERVES 4 (ABOUT 6 CUPS)

8 ounces shiitake mushrooms, cleaned and sliced

2 tablespoons extra-virgin olive oil

Salt and freshly ground black pepper, to taste

Olive oil cooking spray

1 yellow onion, chopped

2 cloves garlic, sliced

2 sprigs fresh thyme

1 cup barley, cooked according to package instructions

1 cup low-sodium chicken stock (or substitute vegetable broth)

3 tablespoons grated parmesan

Kale, Potato,
and Corn Soup

KALE, POTATO, AND CORN SOUP

How about a hale-and-healthy alternative to traditional corn chowder? Potatoes provide the velvety body to this concoction, and the kale's earthy, almost woody flavor balances against the subtle sweetness of the corn. The recipe calls for fresh corn cut right off the cob, which adds a jolt of summery goodness but also makes this a summer soup. If you have a hankering in winter, you can substitute canned plain corn with no salt added.

1. Heat the olive oil in a large saucepan over medium-high heat. Add the onion, carrots, celery, garlic, and thyme. Cook, stirring, until the onion has softened, about 5 minutes.

2. Add the tomato paste and bay leaf and cook for 2 to 3 minutes, stirring, until the paste begins to caramelize. Season with pepper to taste. Add the potatoes and stock and bring to a boil.

3. Reduce the heat to a simmer. Cook covered until the potatoes are soft when pierced with a knife, about 10 minutes. While the potatoes cook, slice the kernels from the corn cobs with a sharp knife.

**SERVES 4 TO 6
(MAKES ABOUT 8 CUPS)**

2 tablespoons extra-virgin olive oil

1 large yellow onion, sliced

2 carrots, diced

2 stalks celery, sliced

3 cloves garlic, chopped

¼ teaspoon dried thyme

1 teaspoon tomato paste

1 small bay leaf

Freshly ground black pepper, to taste

¼ pound new potatoes, quartered

1 quart low-sodium chicken stock (or substitute low-sodium vegetable broth)

2 cobs fresh corn, shucked and cleaned

Continued

4 large leaves kale, woody stems removed and thinly sliced crosswise

Pinch cayenne pepper

Pinch smoked paprika

Parmesan, for serving

4. Add the corn, kale, cayenne, and paprika to the soup and cover. Continue simmering until the corn is cooked through and kale is bright green, about 5 minutes.

5. Add additional pepper and paprika if needed. Ladle the warm soup into bowls and serve, garnished with parmesan cheese if desired.

NUTRITIONAL INFORMATION Per Serving: 199 cal., 7g fat, 1 g sat. fat, 32 g carb., 5 g protein, 168 mg sodium, 6 g sugar, 3 g fiber.

GREEN BEAN AND ARTICHOKE STIR-FRY

It's handy to have a nice vegetarian side dish to offset potatoes or other starches on the table. This one is easy but tastes like a much more complicated dish. The flavors are simple and light but with just enough salty bite to keep things interesting. The quick-cooking method ensures that the green beans maintain not only their ample vitamin C and folates content but also their appealing crunch. The low calories and fat count mean that everyone can dive in for seconds without any guilt.

1. Pour about ½ cup water into a large non-stick skillet (enough to cover the bottom of the pan with water). Add the beans. Bring the water to a simmer over medium-high heat. Cover the pan, and cook for 2 to 3 minutes, or until the beans are bright green.

2. Remove the pan from the heat and toss the beans, until the water is completely evaporated.

3. Add the canola oil and artichokes. Return the pan to the heat and cook, stirring frequently, until the beans begin to char, about 5 minutes.

4. Add the soy sauce and pepper and toss to coat. Remove the pan from the heat, scatter the scallions over the beans and toss to combine.

5. Transfer to a serving bowl and serve warm.

NUTRITIONAL INFORMATION Per Serving: 71 cal., 3 g fat, 0 g sat. fat, 10 g carb., 4 g protein, 131 mg sodium, 0 g sugar, 4 g fiber.

SERVES 4

8 ounces fresh green beans, trimmed and halved

2 teaspoons canola oil

One 9-ounce package frozen artichoke hearts, thawed, drained, and quartered

2 teaspoons low-sodium soy sauce

Freshly ground black pepper, to taste

4 scallions, sliced

ZUCCHINI, CORN, AND PEPPER HASH

Don't be surprised if you find yourself turning to this dish again and again. It's like a warm vegetable salad, full of fresh vegetable crunch and assertive herb flavors. It's a great way to put garden ingredients to work in season, but it's also great to find everything for the hash when the garden isn't in bloom. Best of all, no matter when you pick up the produce, the recipe is heavy on the fiber and nutrients and light on things you don't need like processed sugars and saturated fat. Mix it up as you like by adding the fresh vegetable of your choice.

SERVES 4

1 teaspoon unsalted butter

1 medium yellow onion, chopped

2 cloves garlic, chopped

1 red bell pepper, stemmed, seeded, and chopped

1 medium zucchini, cubed

1 cup corn kernels (canned or frozen)

½ teaspoon dried basil

¼ teaspoon dried thyme

Salt and freshly ground black pepper, to taste

Sweet paprika, for garnish

1. In a large skillet over medium heat, melt the butter. Add the onion, garlic, and bell pepper and cook until softened, 3 to 4 minutes.

2. Add the zucchini, corn, basil, and thyme. Season with salt and pepper to taste and cook, stirring frequently, until the zucchini is soft but not mushy, about 5 minutes.

3. Transfer to a serving bowl, top with a sprinkling of paprika, and serve warm.

NUTRITIONAL INFORMATION Per Serving: 85 cal., 1 g fat, 1 g sat. fat, 16 g carb., 2 g protein, 403 mg sodium, 6 g sugar, 3 g fiber.

HERB-ROASTED PARSNIPS AND CARROTS

When the weather turns a little cold or you're just in the mood for a deep and soulful dish, turn to this classic combo. It can transform a weeknight meal into something special, or go shoulder to shoulder with anything you might put on a holiday table. The secret? A kiss of honey brings out the satisfying earthy sweetness of the root vegetables and gives an already deep and complex mix of flavors something extra. The herbs put this one over the top, but it's the almost smoky, substantial body of the dish that will bring you back for more.

1. Preheat the oven to 400 degrees F. Coat a 9 × 13–inch baking dish with cooking spray.

2. Combine the carrots and parsnips in the baking dish.

3. In a small bowl, whisk together the olive oil, honey, rosemary, and oregano until completely combined. Drizzle the mixture over the vegetables. Toss the vegetables until evenly coated. Season with salt and pepper to taste.

4. Roast until golden brown and soft, 35 to 40 minutes. Turn several times during roasting. (Add 1–2 tablespoons of water if the vegetables stick to the dish.)

5. Transfer the carrots and parsnips to a serving platter, and sprinkle the lemon zest evenly over the vegetables. Serve warm.

NUTRITIONAL INFORMATION Per Serving: 114 cal., 4 g fat, 1 g sat. fat, 19 g carb., 2 g protein, 211 mg sodium, 7 g sugar, 5 g fiber.

SERVES 4

Cooking spray

4 large carrots, peeled and chopped into 1-inch pieces

2 parsnips, peeled and chopped into 1-inch pieces

1 tablespoon extra-virgin olive oil

1 teaspoon honey

½ teaspoon dried rosemary

½ teaspoon dried oregano

Salt and freshly ground black pepper, to taste

Zest of 1 lemon

NUTTY BROWN RICE PILAF

Plain rice pilafs tend to be a bit boring, but there's no law that they have to be. Add the luxuriant magic of toasted nuts and the elegant taste of shallots and you have a great alternative to carb-heavy potatoes. A nut-saturated pilaf such as this goes best with red meat or roasted veal or pork. Or you can go in another direction entirely and pair this lovely side dish with a simple green salad to create a tremendous vegetarian meal that hits all the high notes.

SERVES 4 TO 6

1 tablespoon extra-virgin olive oil

¼ cup sliced almonds

⅓ cup pecan halves, chopped

2 shallots, chopped

1 cup long-grain brown rice

2½ cups low-sodium chicken stock (or substitute vegetable broth)

1 tablespoon dried chives

Salt and freshly ground black pepper, to taste

1. In a large saucepan over medium-low heat, heat the olive oil. Add the almonds and pecans, stirring until the nuts turn golden, about 5 minutes. Transfer the toasted nuts to a paper towel–lined plate to drain.

2. Add the shallots and rice to the pan. Increase the heat to medium. Cook, stirring, until the shallots have softened and the rice is beginning to toast and become fragrant, about 5 minutes.

3. Add the stock, chives, and a small pinch of salt and pepper. Bring to a boil and then reduce the heat to a low simmer. Cover and cook, without stirring, until the liquid is absorbed, about 45 minutes.

4. Remove the pan from the heat and let stand for 10 minutes. Add the nuts and fluff the rice with a fork. Season with salt and pepper to taste. Serve immediately.

NUTRITIONAL INFORMATION Per Serving: 174 cal., 12 g fat, 1 g sat. fat, 14 g carb., 4 g protein, 192 mg sodium, 0 g sugar, 2 g fiber.

ASPARAGUS WITH LEMONY BREADCRUMBS

The tempting tartness of citrus runs all through this dish. Cooking the asparagus with lemon peels bathes the phytonutrient-rich vegetable in the peel's powerful oils. It's a perfect marriage and one made even better with the addition of a layer of breadcrumbs made from whole-grain bread. The rest of the dish is just the basics—fundamental flavors from wholesome ingredients that don't need any help to bring joy to the tongue and stomach alike.

1. Bring a large saucepan of salted water to a boil. Use a vegetable peeler to peel 3 long, wide strips from the lemon and add them to the water. Reserve the rest of the lemon. Add the asparagus and cook until fork-tender, 3 to 5 minutes. Drain and set aside.

2. While the asparagus is cooking, heat the olive oil in a small skillet over medium-low heat. Add the fresh breadcrumbs and season with a pinch of salt and a dash of freshly ground black pepper. Stir until the bread is evenly golden and crisp.

3. Remove the pan from the heat. Zest half of the lemon over the crumbs. Reserve the rest of the lemon. Let cool.

4. Transfer the asparagus to a serving platter and crumble the breadcrumbs over top. Slice the remaining lemon in half, squeeze lemon juice over the asparagus, and serve.

NUTRITIONAL INFORMATION Per Serving: 87 cal., 4 g fat, 1 g sat. fat, 15 g carb., 2 g protein, 182 mg sodium, 1 g sugar, 2 g fiber.

SERVES 4

1 lemon

1 pound asparagus, trimmed

1 teaspoon extra-virgin olive oil

1 slice whole-grain bread, torn into very small pieces

Salt and freshly ground black pepper, to taste

STEAMED SESAME BOK CHOY

Bok choy, like other members of the cabbage family, is chock-full of nutrients and compounds that can help the heart, stomach, and more. Chances are, however, that you'll be thinking more about the piquant flavors than your next checkup when you whip up this easy, fast, and fantastically delicious side dish. Steaming maintains any green's character, keeping a bit of the crunch and many more of the nutrients than other methods of cooking. A few classic Asian ingredients add flavor fireworks without introducing sugars or fats. Throw in a scattering of chopped, broiled chicken breast to create a stunning low-cal main course.

SERVES 4

1 pound baby bok choy, halved through the core

1 tablespoon rice vinegar

1 teaspoon toasted sesame oil

½ teaspoon sesame seeds

Pinch chili flakes, optional

1. Add about 1 inch of water to a large saucepan and fit it with a steamer insert or basket. Bring the water to a boil over medium-high heat.

2. Add the bok choy, cover, and steam until a knife inserted into the core meets little resistance, about 5 minutes. Using tongs, transfer the bok choy to a serving platter.

3. While the bok choy cooks, whisk the vinegar, sesame oil, sesame seeds, and chili flakes (if using) together in a small bowl. Drizzle the dressing over the warm bok choy and serve warm or at room temperature.

NUTRITIONAL INFORMATION Per Serving: 26 cal., 0 g fat, 0 g sat. fat, 6 g carb., 0 g protein, 40 mg sodium, 0 g sugar, 0 g fiber.

CHILE-LIME SWEET POTATOES

Unusual flavor combinations are great for breaking you out of your culinary routine and injecting a whole lot of excitement into any meal. You'll look long and hard to find a mix of flavors quite as exciting and intriguing as the ones in this dish. Tangy and hot play against the understated sweetness of the tuber, making more of the sweet potatoes than your tongue would have thought possible. It's an innovative and adaptable approach; you can substitute potatoes, yams, parsnips, and even beets if you're not a big fan of sweet potatoes.

1. Add ½ inch of water to a large saucepan. Set a vegetable steamer basket inside the pot and bring the water to a boil over medium-high heat.

2. Add the sweet potatoes. Cover and cook until soft but still holding their shape, 15 to 20 minutes. A knife inserted into a potato should meet no resistance.

3. Transfer the potatoes to a serving bowl and drizzle with the olive oil and lime juice. Toss gently to coat. Season with the chili powder, salt, and pepper and serve warm.

NUTRITIONAL INFORMATION Per Serving: 128 cal., 7 g fat, 1 g sat. fat, 14 g carb., 1 g protein, 193 mg sodium, 3 g sugar, 2 g fiber.

SERVES 4

2 large sweet potatoes, peeled and cut into 1-inch cubes

2 teaspoons extra-virgin olive oil

Juice of ½ lime

¼ teaspoon chili powder, or to taste

Salt and freshly ground black pepper, to taste

CAULIFLOWER STEAKS WITH TOMATO RELISH

Cauliflower, like many of its cruciferous cousins, offers a wealth of health benefits. This snow-white vegetable has been shown to contain compounds linked with cancer prevention, inflammation-fighting, cholesterol reduction, and more. The problem is that plain old cauliflower can be a bit boring—but not if you prepare it in a whole new and unexpected way. Cut "steaks" from the vegetable and you make it more interesting from the get-go. Inject a bit of tangy and salty flavors into the cauliflower and cook it just right so that it has a little roasted goodness and you've got a side dish that can't be beat.

SERVES 4

1 large head cauliflower, trimmed

Olive oil cooking spray

Salt and freshly ground black pepper, to taste

1 small red onion, finely chopped

1 tablespoon capers, drained

1 vine-ripened tomato, seeded and diced

1 teaspoon honey

1 teaspoon red wine vinegar

1. Preheat the oven to 450 degrees F. Line a baking sheet with parchment paper.

2. Set the cauliflower head upright on a cutting board and cut it in half through the core. Very carefully cut each half into ½-inch slices vertically through the core.

3. Coat the lined baking sheet with cooking spray and arrange the cauliflower slices in a single layer. Spray the slices with the cooking spray, and season them well with salt and pepper.

4. Roast the cauliflower until it turns golden and the edges are beginning to brown, about 10 minutes. Carefully flip the slices with a spatula and continue roasting until golden brown and soft when pierced with a knife, about 10 minutes more. Remove from the oven and let cool briefly on the pan.

5. While the cauliflower cooks, spray a small saucepan with the cooking spray and heat it over medium heat. Add the onion and stir until softened, about 4 minutes.

6. Add the capers and tomato. Stir frequently until the tomatoes are just beginning to break down, about 5 minutes. Add the honey and vinegar, and cook until the liquid has evaporated, 2 to 3 minutes.

7. Season with salt and pepper to taste. Remove the pan from the heat.

8. Arrange the cauliflower on a serving platter and scatter the relish over the top. Serve warm.

NUTRITIONAL INFORMATION Per Serving: 54 cal., 0 g fat, 0 g sat. fat, 12 g carb., 3 g protein, 264 mg sodium, 6 g sugar, 4 g fiber.

CUCUMBER GAZPACHO

Tomato gazpacho is the more common version, but if more people discover the sparkling, refreshing flavors in this elegant soup, that won't be the case much longer. This version of the famed Spanish soup takes advantage of the English cucumber, featuring a lighter, more floral, and more complex flavor than slicing cucumbers. Its hint of sweetness plays well against the shaper, tangy flavors of citrus and vinegar, and makes every spoonful a reviving delight.

SERVES 4 (MAKES ABOUT 6 CUPS)

1 English cucumber, peeled and chopped

1 small yellow bell pepper, stemmed, seeded, and chopped

2 scallions, chopped

1 small clove garlic, smashed

½ cup plain nonfat Greek yogurt

1 cup low-fat buttermilk

1 teaspoon white vinegar

Juice of ½ lemon

Salt and freshly ground black pepper, to taste

Sliced almonds, toasted, for garnish

Chopped fresh mint, for garnish

1. Combine the cucumber, bell pepper, scallions, garlic, yogurt, buttermilk, vinegar, and lemon juice in the canister of a blender. Blend until liquefied.

2. Season with salt and pepper to taste. If the soup is too thick, thin with cold water.

3. Serve the soup cold garnished with almonds and mint.

NUTRITIONAL INFORMATION Per Serving: 61 cal., 4 g fat, 1 g sat. fat, 10 g carb., 5 g protein, 226 mg sodium, 4 g sugar, 2 g fiber.

SPICY CARROT AND CELERY ROOT SOUP

The carrot is a great base for a soup, at once lightly sweet, and silky when puréed. But the big bang in a bowl full of this soup is the celery root. It also cooks up beautifully, with a stronger flavor than celery. The real plus, though, is that the root is packed with vitamins, carotene, and other nutrients and is touted for its analgesic, anti-allergenic, and therapeutic traits. Add a few zippy spices and great health never tasted so good.

1. Heat the olive oil in a large saucepan over medium heat. Add the shallots and garlic and cook until softened, about 5 minutes. Add the ginger and jalapeño and stir well.

2. Add the carrots, celery root, and orange juice and bring to a simmer. Stir until the liquid has reduced slightly, 2 to 3 minutes.

3. Add the vegetable broth and bring the mixture to a boil. Reduce the heat to medium-low, cover, and cook until the carrots and celery root are completely soft and falling apart, 30 to 40 minutes.

4. Working in batches, purée the soup in a blender or with a handheld immersion blender. Return the soup to the pan. Season with lemon juice and pepper to taste.

5. Ladle the soup into bowls, garnish with scallions and serve warm.

NUTRITIONAL INFORMATION Per Serving: 175 cal., 5 g fat, 1 g sat. fat, 30 g carb., 3 g protein, 326 mg sodium, 7 g sugar, 5 g fiber.

SERVES 4 (MAKES ABOUT 6 CUPS)

1 tablespoon extra-virgin olive oil

2 large shallots, chopped

2 cloves garlic, smashed

1 tablespoon grated fresh, peeled ginger

½ small jalapeño, seeded and chopped

3 large carrots, peeled and chopped

1 medium celery root, peeled and roughly chopped

½ cup orange juice

1 quart low-sodium vegetable broth

Freshly ground black pepper, to taste

Juice of 1 lemon

4 scallions, sliced, for garnish

Dilled Tuna and
Chickpea Salad Sandwiches

DILLED TUNA AND CHICKPEA SALAD SANDWICHES

You'll find this creation at the crossroads where terrific flavor meets perfect protein. Plain old tuna salad sandwiches can't hold a candle to a version that has been blessed with a helping of dill and a sturdy, smooth consistency courtesy of mashed chickpeas. Small accents of onion, mustard, citrus, and pepper boost the natural flavor of the tuna and make this a wonderful sandwich for a lunch, snack, picnic, or even a make-ahead weeknight meal.

1. Mash the chickpeas in a medium bowl with a potato masher. Add the tuna and flake it with a fork to break it up. Add the celery and shallots and toss to combine.

2. In a small bowl, combine the yogurt, mustard, lime juice, and dill and stir to incorporate. Add this mixture to the tuna and toss gently to mix. Season with pepper to taste.

3. Arrange the 4 slices of the toasted bread on a work surface and cover each with a lettuce leaf. Divide the tuna salad among the bread slices, lay a tomato slice on top and assemble the top slice.

4. Press the sandwiches lightly, slice them on the diagonal, and serve.

NUTRITIONAL INFORMATION Per Serving: 229 cal., 3 g fat, 0 g sat. fat, 27 g carb., 22 g protein, 436 mg sodium, 4 g sugar, 4 g fiber.

SERVES 4

½ cup canned chickpeas, drained

Two 6-ounce cans all-white tuna packed in water, drained

1 celery stalk, finely diced

1 small shallot, finely diced

½ cup nonfat plain Greek yogurt

1 teaspoon Dijon mustard

Juice of 1 lime

2 tablespoons minced fresh dill (or substitute 2 teaspoons dried)

Freshly ground black pepper, to taste

8 slices light whole-grain sandwich bread, toasted

4 pieces green leaf lettuce

4 thin slices beefsteak tomato

Pan-Seared Citrus Chicken

PAN-SEARED CITRUS CHICKEN

Add a Caribbean splash to your next chicken meal with a bright combination of citrus sections and juices. The trio of grapefruit, orange, and lime join forces to create an exceptional marinade that will make each bit of your chicken burst with sun-filled flavor. Pan-searing is an ideal way to cook these breasts because it seals in the juices—and the citrus flavors—and adds a lovely char to the bird's surface.

1. Using a sharp knife, halve the chicken breasts horizontally. Transfer the chicken to a resealable plastic bag and add the grapefruit, orange, and lime juices; 1 tablespoon of the olive oil; the garlic; and thyme. Squeeze the chicken around in the bag with your hands to mix the marinade. Refrigerate for at least 15 minutes and no longer than 30 minutes.

2. Heat the remaining olive oil in a nonstick skillet over medium heat, swirling to coat the pan. Using tongs, remove the chicken pieces from the bag and shake off the excess marinade. Discard the marinade. Add the chicken to the skillet and season with salt and pepper.

3. Cook the chicken pieces without moving them until the undersides are golden, about 5 minutes. Flip them, season with salt and pepper, and cook until the bottoms are golden brown, another 4 to 5 minutes.

SERVES 4

2 large skinless, boneless chicken-breast halves (about 1 pound)

¼ cup fresh grapefruit juice

Juice of ½ orange

Juice of ½ lime

2 tablespoons extra-virgin olive oil

2 cloves garlic, smashed

1 sprig fresh thyme

Salt and freshly ground black pepper, to taste

4. Check with an internal-read thermometer—the internal temperature should be at least 165 degrees F. If not, cover and continue cooking until the chicken is cooked through. Let the chicken rest for a couple of minutes before slicing and serving.

NUTRITIONAL INFORMATION Per Serving: 224 cal., 9 g fat, 1 g sat. fat, 26 g carb., 29 g protein, 241 mg sodium, 1 g sugar, 0 g fiber.

Turkey, Apple, and
Cheddar Panini

TURKEY, APPLE, AND CHEDDAR PANINI

Paninis are just plain fun. Fun to make and even more fun to eat. This panini is no exception. It includes that classic marriage of apple and cheddar that makes apple pie such an all-time favorite. Trap those two with turkey and you really have something special. The understated flavor of the meat lets the apple and cheese shine through. The ciabatta brings an added element of subtle sweetness and a chewy character that holds up well to the heat.

SERVES 4

1 tablespoon extra-virgin olive oil

4 turkey cutlets (about 1 pound)

Freshly ground black pepper, to taste

2 tablespoons whole-grain mustard

4 light multigrain English muffins, halved

4 slices reduced-fat, cheddar-cheese sandwich slices

2 cups arugula leaves

1 Gala apple, cored and thinly sliced (or substitute Honeycrisp)

1. Heat the olive oil in a large nonstick skillet over medium-high heat. Season the turkey cutlets on both sides with pepper. Cook, turning once, until light golden brown and cooked through, 3 to 4 minutes per side. Remove from the heat.

2. Spread mustard on both sides of each English muffin and lay a slice of cheese on each half. Put the turkey cutlets on the roll bottoms, followed by one-quarter of the arugula.

3. Arrange the apple slices in a single layer over the arugula and set the English muffin tops on the apples.

4. Wipe any residue from the pan with a paper towel. Heat the pan over medium-low heat.

5. Arrange the sandwiches in the pan (work in batches if necessary). Cover them with a sheet of aluminum foil and rest another large skillet or stock pot directly on top of the sandwiches to weigh them down.

6. Cook for 3 to 4 minutes, until the English muffin bottoms are golden. Remove the top pan and foil, and flip the sandwiches with tongs. Replace the foil and pan, and cook until the cheese is melted, 2 to 3 minutes more.

7. Remove the sandwiches from the pan. Let them rest for a minute or two. Slice each and serve warm.

NUTRITIONAL INFORMATION Per Serving: 318 cal., 9 g fat, 1 g sat. fat, 38 g carb., 38 g protein, 426 mg sodium, 4 g sugar, 9 g fiber.

PORK TENDERLOIN SANDWICH

WITH ARTICHOKE SPREAD

Pork tenderloin is a terrific burger substitute because it's not only lighter tasting and less filling, it's also much healthier. That said, this sandwich is about the lean sweet flavor of the meat and how it goes so well with the luscious savory treat that is the artichoke spread.

SERVES 4

1 pork tenderloin (about 1 pound), sliced diagonally into 4 equal-sized pieces

Freshly ground black pepper, to taste

Cooking spray

¼ cup marinated artichoke hearts, drained

6 large pitted green olives

1 small shallot, minced

½ teaspoon honey

4 red leaf lettuce leaves

8 slices light whole-wheat bread

1 beefsteak tomato, thinly sliced

1. Use a meat mallet to pound each pork piece between 2 sheets of plastic, until each is about ⅛-inch thick. Season on both sides with pepper.

2. Heat a stovetop grill pan over medium-high heat. Mist it with cooking spray. Grill the pork, turning once, until grill marks appear and the pork is cooked through, about 2 minutes per side.

3. While the pork cooks, combine the artichoke hearts, olives, shallot, and honey in the bowl of a food processor. Pulse until a rough paste forms. If the paste is dry, add about a teaspoon of the marinade from the artichoke jar and mix well.

4. Spread a thin layer of the artichoke spread on the slices of bread. Place a lettuce leaf on each bottom, topped by a piece of pork, some tomato slices, and the top slice. Serve immediately.

NUTRITIONAL INFORMATION Per Serving: 274 cal., 9 g fat, 2 g sat. fat, 22 g carb., 29 g protein, 435 mg sodium, 3 g sugar, 5 g fiber.

ENERGIZING AVOCADO-CHICKEN SALAD

You'd be hard-pressed to find a more trouble-free, easy, combine-and-serve salad. That's not to say there's any lack of exciting flavors here. Quite the opposite. You'll enjoy a little sweet, a little tart, a little tangy, and much, much more. The energy in this salad comes from the high-octane texture and burst of usable sugars and calories. There's a bunch of crunch in this unique salad, providing some snap between in every bite and reinforcing the impression of ultimate freshness with just the hint of smokiness from the rotisserie chicken. Make extra because you'll want more for later!

1. In a large bowl, combine the celery, salt, pepper, mayonnaise, lime juice, and olive oil. Whisk until thoroughly incorporated. Add the chicken to the bowl and toss to coat.

2. Add the avocado and apple and mix with a fork, being careful not to smash them. Divide the salad among four plates and garnish each with 3 chips.

NUTRITIONAL INFORMATION Per Serving: 330 cal., 21 g fat, 3 g sat. fat, 17 g carb., 19 g protein, 320 mg sodium, 4 g sugar, 5 g fiber.

SERVES 4

¼ cup diced celery

¼ teaspoon salt

⅛ teaspoon freshly ground black pepper

¼ cup low-fat mayonnaise

2 tablespoons fresh lime juice

1 tablespoon olive oil

2 cups shredded, skinless, boneless rotisserie-chicken breast

1 ripe avocado, peeled and chopped

1 cup chopped apple

12 tortilla chips

Orzo Salad with Shrimp,
Cucumbers, and Feta

ORZO SALAD WITH SHRIMP, CUCUMBERS, AND FETA

Although orzo is the Italian word for "barley," it's also a wonderful, rice-shaped pasta. Orzo is chewy, with a lot of flavor-grabbing surface area. That comes in handy for capturing the cascade of perky, garden-fresh flavors in this salad. The shrimp brings a delicate sweetness to the party, and the citrus makes everything else sparkle.

1. In a medium saucepan over medium-high heat, combine 2 cups water with the lemon peel, half of the lemon juice, the garlic, and peppercorns and bring to a boil.

2. Remove the pan from the heat, stir in the shrimp, and cover. Let stand until the shrimp are cooked through and opaque, about 5 minutes.

3. Drain the shrimp. Discard the cooking water ingredients and let the shrimp cool to room temperature.

4. In a mixing bowl, combine the orzo, cucumber, dill, and shrimp and toss. In another small bowl, combine the remaining lemon juice and olive oil. Whisk until emulsified and season with pepper to taste.

5. Add the dressing to the orzo and sprinkle with the crumbled cheese. Toss gently until the dressing is absorbed. Serve chilled or at room temperature.

NUTRITIONAL INFORMATION Per Serving: 277 cal., 14 g fat, 5 g sat. fat, 44 g carb., 18 g protein, 372 mg sodium, 3 g sugar, 2 g fiber.

SERVES 4

3 large strips lemon peel

Juice of 1 lemon

1 clove garlic, smashed

12 whole black peppercorns

12 ounces medium shrimp (41–50), shelled, and deveined

1 cup orzo pasta, cooked according to package instructions and rinsed

½ English cucumber, diced

¼ cup chopped fresh dill

2 tablespoons light olive oil

Freshly ground black pepper, to taste

4 ounces crumbled feta cheese

GREENS AND GRAINS SALAD

If you're looking for maximum nutrients in a palate-pleasing dish, you can't really go wrong by combining some fiber-rich grains with nutrient-dense lettuce standouts. The cast of this salad stars unusual grains from around the world, with nuts and a bevy of interesting greens.

SERVES 4

½ cup bulgur wheat, cooked according to package instructions

½ cup barley, cooked according to package instructions

½ cup farro, cooked according to package instructions

⅓ cup slivered almonds, toasted

2 heads endive, sliced crosswise into ¼-inch strips and separated

1 small head radicchio, sliced

1 romaine heart, chopped into ½-inch ribbons

1 tablespoon sherry vinegar

1 teaspoon Dijon mustard

1 small shallot, minced

2 tablespoons extra-virgin olive oil

Pinch dried thyme

Pinch dried oregano

Salt and freshly ground black pepper, to taste

4 scallions, sliced

Shaved pecorino romano, for garnish

1. In a medium bowl, combine the bulgur, barley, farro, and almonds. In a large, shallow serving bowl or platter, combine the endive, radicchio, and romaine and toss.

2. In a small bowl, combine the vinegar, mustard, and shallots. Whisk until incorporated. Add the olive oil, thyme, and oregano, and whisk until thick and emulsified. Season with salt and pepper to taste.

3. Pour half of the dressing over the mixed grains. Add the scallions, and toss until evenly dressed.

4. Pour the remaining dressing over the greens and toss to coat. Scatter the grains over the greens, garnish with shaved pecorino romano, and serve on a single platter.

NUTRITIONAL INFORMATION Per Serving: 243 cal., 14 g fat, 2 g sat. fat, 17 g carb., 8 g protein, 413 mg sodium, 2 g sugar, 11 g fiber.

Greens and
Grains Salad

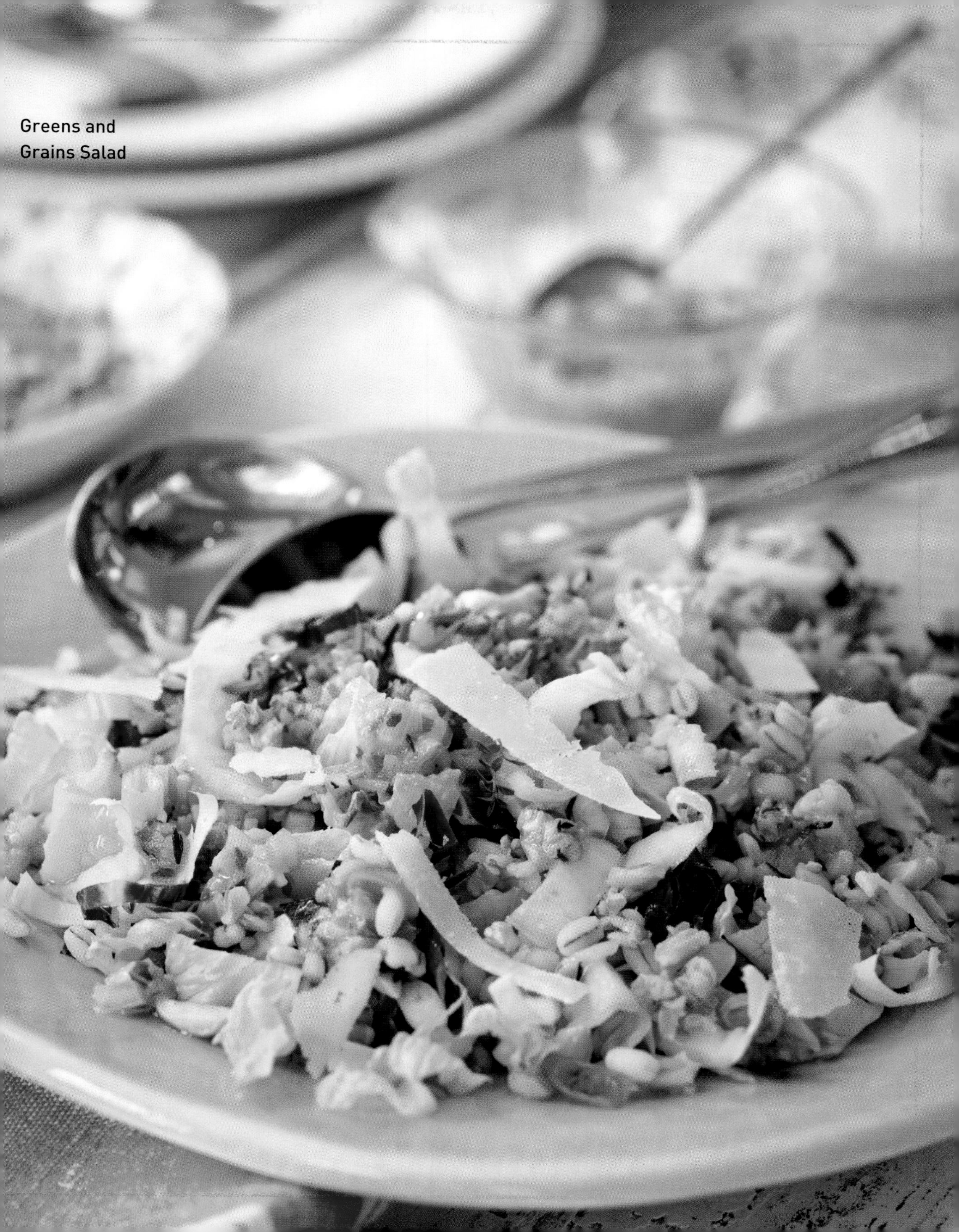

Tomato and
Mozzarella Salad

TOMATO AND MOZZARELLA SALAD

WITH SMOKED PAPRIKA VINAIGRETTE

This is a bit of an update on the popular caprese salad, that simple Italian combo of olive oil, tomatoes, and buffalo mozzarella. This version includes a nice bit of salty goodness in the form of the vaunted Greek Kalamata olives and a rich note courtesy of smoked paprika. Making the salad with a reduced-fat mozzarella ensures it stays healthy, and the many flavors guarantee that you won't miss the fat at all.

1. Arrange the tomatoes on a serving platter and season them lightly with pepper. Scatter the chopped olives over the tomatoes.

2. In a small bowl, combine the vinegar, olive oil, and smoked paprika. Whisk until integrated. Season with pepper to taste.

3. Drizzle the dressing over the tomatoes. Scatter the cheese over the top of the salad and garnish with the basil. Serve at room temperature.

NUTRITIONAL INFORMATION Per Serving: 167 cal., 9 g fat, 3 g sat. fat, 9 g carb., 5 g protein, 351 mg sodium, 0 g sugar, 1 g fiber.

SERVES 4

4 heirloom tomatoes, (about 1½ pounds), sliced into bite-sized wedges

Freshly ground black pepper, to taste

¼ cup pitted Kalamata olives, coarsely chopped

2 teaspoons white wine vinegar

2 tablespoons extra-virgin olive oil

¼ teaspoon smoked paprika

2 ounces reduced-fat mozzarella cheese, cut into thin matchsticks

6 large fresh basil leaves, thinly sliced

ROASTED BEETS

WITH ARUGULA, PISTACHIOS, AND LEMON-SCENTED RICOTTA

Beets were the original culinary sweetener because of their high sugar content. Roasting accentuates that sweetness, elevating it and combining it with a hint of smokiness—both of which contrast the tangier notes of lemon and vinegar in this dish. That dynamic tension between tart and sweet is what makes this vegetarian option so compelling. Throw in the lovely texture of ricotta and you have a show-stopping lunch, meatless dinner, or side dish.

SERVES 4

1 medium red onion, sliced into 4 thick rounds

4 large beets, scrubbed

1 tablespoon extra-virgin olive oil

2 teaspoons balsamic vinegar

Zest of 1 lemon

½ cup low-fat ricotta cheese

Salt and freshly ground black pepper, to taste

6 cups baby arugula leaves

1 teaspoon lemon juice

¼ cup shelled roasted pistachios

1. Preheat the oven to 400 degrees F.

2. Lay four 12-inch squares of aluminum foil on a work surface. Set an onion slice on each foil sheet and rest a beet on each onion. Drizzle olive oil and vinegar over each, and wrap them in the foil.

3. Place the packets on a baking sheet and roast in the center of the oven until a knife inserted into the beets meets little resistance, 1 to 1 ¼ hours. Remove from the oven and let stand until cool enough to handle.

4. Unwrap the packets. Use a paper towel to rub the skins off of each beet. Slice the beets into wedges and place them in a bowl. Sprinkle with the remaining vinegar and toss until coated. Separate the roasted onion slices into rings.

5. In a small bowl, fold the lemon zest into the cheese and season lightly with salt and pepper.

6. Spread the arugula on a serving platter. Scatter the roasted onion rings over the greens and sprinkle the lemon juice over the top. Season with salt and pepper and toss lightly to dress the greens.

7. Arrange the beets on top of the greens. Use 2 spoons to drop dollops of the lemony ricotta all over the salad. Scatter the pistachios over the top and serve.

NUTRITIONAL INFORMATION Per Serving: 145 cal., 5 g fat, 1 g sat. fat, 18 g carb., 9 g protein, 294 mg sodium, 10 g sugar, 4 g fiber.

GRAPEFRUIT AND HEARTS OF PALM SALAD

WITH HONEY-LIME VINAIGRETTE

Love artichoke hearts? Then you'll love hearts of palm even more. They have a clean, refreshing flavor, with an alluring moistness and a hearty snap between the teeth. Grapefruit is a perfectly suited companion, with a vibrant natural sweetness that mingles seamlessly with the simple, satisfying taste of the hearts of palm. All you need is a light coating of lime-based vinaigrette for a salad with a wake-me-up zip that will make your day.

SERVES 4

2 large ruby grapefruit

One 14-ounce can hearts of palm, drained and sliced

2 heads endive, sliced crosswise

Salt and freshly ground black pepper, to taste

Juice of 1 lime

½ teaspoon Dijon mustard

1 teaspoon honey

2 tablespoons extra-virgin olive oil

⅓ cup fresh flat-leaf parsley leaves

1. Rest a grapefruit on a cutting board, top-side down. Use a sharp knife to cut away the peel and pith (white part) from around the outside of the fruit. Very carefully cut the flesh segments away from the membrane that separates them. Repeat with the other grapefruit. Spread the grapefruit segments across a serving platter.

2. Add the hearts of palm and endive to the platter and gently toss. Season the salad lightly with salt and pepper.

3. In a small bowl, combine the lime juice, mustard, honey, and olive oil. Whisk until thick and emulsified. Season the dressing with salt and pepper and drizzle it evenly over the salad. Scatter the parsley leaves on top and serve.

NUTRITIONAL INFORMATION Per Serving: 202 cal., 8 g fat, 1 g sat. fat, 26 g carb., 8 g protein, 660 mg sodium, 1 g sugar, 14 g fiber.

BABY SPINACH SALAD

WITH CRISPY SHALLOTS AND SMOKED GOUDA

This salad is all about deep, earthy flavors. The fresh, strong vegetable essence of raw baby spinach. The smoky appeal of carefully roasted shallots. The unadulterated richness of smoked Gouda. Combine all those on a single plate and you have something very special—the type of meal that offers delight for the tongue and indulgence for the soul. This creation is also healthy as can be, full of vitamins and minerals thanks to the greens.

1. Preheat the oven to 375 degrees F. Line a baking sheet with parchment paper.

2. Spread the shallots in a single layer across the baking sheet. Spray them with the cooking spray and toss to coat. Bake, tossing them occasionally with a spatula, until they begin to brown and crisp, about 15 minutes. Check often; they will turn bitter if they darken too much. Remove from the oven and let cool.

2. In a large serving bowl, combine the spinach and tomatoes and toss. In a small bowl, combine the vinegar and mustard and stir to mix. Add the olive oil and whisk until thick and emulsified. Season with salt and pepper to taste.

3. Scatter the shallots over the spinach and drizzle the dressing over the salad. Toss gently to combine and coat the spinach. Scatter the cheese over the top and serve.

NUTRITIONAL INFORMATION Per Serving: 167 cal., 12 g fat, 4 g sat. fat, 7 g carb., 6 g protein, 342 mg sodium, 2 g sugar, 3 g fiber.

SERVES 4

3 large shallots, sliced into thin rings and separated

Olive oil cooking spray

8 cups baby spinach leaves

1 cup grape tomatoes, quartered

2 teaspoons red wine vinegar

1 teaspoon whole-grain Dijon mustard

2 tablespoons extra-virgin olive oil

Salt and freshly ground black pepper, to taste

2 ounces smoked Gouda cheese, finely diced

UNCLE JOHNNY'S BLACK-EYED PEA SALAD

This has always been one of my family's favorite side dishes, one that can be pulled into the center of the plate for a main course. Black-eyed peas are one of the meatiest vegetables around, and in Southern tradition they are good luck if eaten on New Year's Eve or New Year's Day. Uncle Johnny came up with this recipe as something light and balanced and flavorful. Like everything else he cooks, he whips this up with ease and grace.

SERVES 4

½ cup olive oil

Juice of ½ lemon

⅛ cup vinegar

Pinch of sugar

Salt and freshly ground black pepper, to taste

One 16-ounce can black-eyed peas, drained and rinsed

2–3 scallions, trimmed and chopped

3–4 tablespoons chopped fresh flat-leaf parsley

1 small yellow onion, chopped

½ cup chopped red pepper

½ cup chopped green pepper

1 tablespoon chopped red onion

1 tablespoon chopped chives

1 cup chopped fresh tomato

1 cup chopped cucumber

1 cup chopped celery

Shredded lettuce, for serving

1. In a small bowl, combine the olive oil, lemon juice, vinegar, and pinch of sugar. Whisk until the dressing is thick and emulsified. Season with salt and pepper to taste.

2. In a large serving bowl, whisk together the remaining ingredients except for the lettuce. Toss to mix.

3. Drizzle the dressing over the salad and toss until well coated. Let stand approximately 15 minutes before serving. Season with additional salt and pepper to taste.

4. Serve on a bed of shredded lettuce.

NUTRITIONAL INFORMATION Per Serving: 156 cal., 28 g fat, 4 g sat. fat, 40 g carb., 12 g protein, 72 mg sodium, 17 g sugar, 16 g fiber.

Uncle Johnny's
Black-Eyed Pea
Salad

MEAT-PACKING PEPPERS

These could just as easily have been called protein-packing peppers. The beef is lean but serves as a rich stage for all the other ingredients, and what a production. It's a balanced blend of scintillating flavors and textures that just begs to be eaten—there's a reason why stuffed peppers have been a regular in the kitchen rotation since grandma's day. Filling, wholesome ingredients provide a thrill for every part of your tongue. Whether you serve it as a weeknight meal or put it on the table for Sunday family dinner, nobody will walk away hungry.

SERVES 4

4 large red bell peppers (or use a combination of colors)

1 tablespoon olive oil

1 pound lean ground beef

1 medium onion, chopped

2 cloves garlic, minced

1 teaspoon chili powder

1 teaspoon dried oregano

1 teaspoon brown mustard

½ teaspoon onion powder

Freshly ground pepper, to taste

One-half (14.5 ounce) can diced tomatoes

One 8-ounce can no-salt-added tomato sauce

4 tablespoons tomato paste

1. Preheat the broiler. Line a roasting pan with aluminum foil. Set the oven rack about 8 inches from the heat source, if possible.

2. Bring a large pot of water to boil over high heat. Cut the tops off the bell peppers and remove the seeds and membranes. Rinse the peppers under cold water.

3. Add the bell peppers to the pot, reduce the heat, and simmer for 5 minutes, or until tender. Drain and set the peppers aside.

4. In a large skillet over medium-high heat, heat ½ tablespoon of the olive oil. Brown the beef. Remove the beef with slotted spoon and set aside.

5. Pour out the excess grease from the skillet and heat the skillet over medium-high heat. Add the remaining olive oil.

6. Add the onion and garlic. Stir until softened and fragrant, 2 to 3 minutes. Add the chili powder, oregano, mustard, and onion powder, and stir to coat the vegetables. Season with pepper to taste.

7. Add the tomatoes, tomato sauce, and tomato paste. Stir to combine and simmer for 3 to 4 minutes. Add the meat and simmer until heated through.

8. Fill the bell peppers with the beef mixture and place them upright in the roasting pan. Broil for 3 to 5 minutes until heated through.

NUTRITIONAL INFORMATION Per Serving: 305 cal., 9 g fat, 3 g sat. fat, 24 g carb., 27 g protein, 239 mg sodium, 14 g sugar, 4 g fiber.

CHICKPEA AND CELERY SALAD

WITH LEMON-PARMESAN DRESSING

Some salads have stars, but this one features a delicious ensemble cast. It's a tumble of flavors and textures that looks great on the plate. What unites all these varied ingredients is a just-picked freshness, and there is something for every part of your tongue—smooth, sweet, tart, even a little umami. But the real attraction is a wealth of protein, fiber, vitamins, and other nutrients throughout this salad. It doesn't hurt that it's easy and quick to make.

SERVES 4

4 celery stalks, sliced diagonally, plus the leaves

One 15-ounce can chickpeas, drained and rinsed

1 large head frisée, roughly chopped

1 bunch chives, sliced

1 tablespoon fresh lemon juice

1 teaspoon Dijon mustard

½ teaspoon honey

1 tablespoon grated parmesan

2 tablespoons extra-virgin olive oil

Freshly ground black pepper, to taste

¼ cup roasted, salted sunflower seeds

1. In a large serving bowl or salad platter, combine the sliced celery, chickpeas, frisée, and chives. Toss to mix.

2. In a small bowl, combine the lemon juice, mustard, and honey and whisk to incorporate. Add the parmesan and olive oil and whisk until thick and emulsified. Season with pepper to taste.

3. Drizzle the dressing over the salad and toss until well coated. Season with a little more black pepper to taste. Coarsely chop the celery leaves and scatter them over the top along with the sunflower seeds and more grated parmesan, if desired. Serve immediately.

NUTRITIONAL INFORMATION Per Serving: 262 cal., 14 g fat, 1 g sat. fat, 28 g carb., 6 g protein, 627 mg sodium, 0 g sugar, 6 g fiber.

QUINOA WITH DANDELION GREENS, APPLES, AND PECANS

Surprising flavor combinations are often the most interesting for a salad. That's what makes this dish work so well; the pleasantly bitter and earthy dandelion greens wouldn't be the first ingredient that most people would pick to go with a light grain like quinoa, but the combo works wonderfully. The apples and pecans inject a touch of sweetness and richness so that the savory flavors aren't overwhelming. It's an interesting mixture from the first forkful to the last.

1. Combine the quinoa, greens, pecans, and apples in a large serving bowl and toss to mix.

2. In a medium bowl, whisk together the vinegar, garlic powder, thyme, and mustard. Add the olive oil, season with salt and pepper as needed, and whisk until thick and emulsified.

3. Add the dressing to the salad and toss to coat. Serve.

NUTRITIONAL INFORMATION Per Serving: 355 cal., 17 g fat, 2 g sat. fat, 43 g carb., 8 g protein, 204 mg sodium, 9 g sugar, 5 g fiber.

SERVES 4

1 cup quinoa, cooked according to package instructions

1 small bunch dandelion greens, thinly sliced crosswise

⅓ cup pecans, toasted and coarsely chopped

2 Gala apples, cored and diced (or substitute Honeycrisp)

2 teaspoons cider vinegar

Pinch garlic powder

Pinch dried thyme

1 teaspoon Dijon mustard

2 tablespoons extra-virgin olive oil

Salt and freshly ground black pepper, to taste

Butter Lettuce with
Oranges, Olives,
and Tarragon Vinaigrette

BUTTER LETTUCE WITH ORANGES, OLIVES,
AND TARRAGON VINAIGRETTE

Butter lettuce boasts one of the most appealing flavors among leafy greens—ever so slightly sweet with a clean finish. It's right at home in the balance between sweet and salty salad ingredients. The most interesting and flavor-packed salads play off that balance, and this vibrant lunch special makes the most of it. The almost candy sweetness of ripe oranges counters the salty olives. A simple dressing allows the contrasts to shine at their most delicious.

1. Spread the lettuce on a serving platter. Divide each orange in half using the segments as a guide. Slice the orange halves crosswise into half-moon slices and arrange them on top of the lettuce. Scatter the olives and almonds over the salad.

2. In a small bowl, whisk together the vinegar, mustard, tarragon, and shallot until combined. Add the olive oil, season with salt and pepper as needed, and whisk until thick and emulsified.

3. Drizzle the dressing over the salad, garnish with parmesan shavings and serve.

NUTRITIONAL INFORMATION Per Serving: 206 cal., 12 g fat, 1 g sat. fat, 15 g carb., 4 g protein, 444 mg sodium, 7 g sugar, 3 g fiber.

SERVES 4

1 large head butter lettuce, torn into bite-sized pieces

2 navel oranges, peeled

¼ cup pitted Kalamata olives, chopped

⅓ cup sliced almonds, toasted

1 tablespoon white wine vinegar

½ teaspoon whole-grain Dijon mustard

2 teaspoons chopped fresh tarragon

2 teaspoons finely minced shallot

2 tablespoons extra-virgin olive oil

Salt and freshly ground black pepper, to taste

Shaved parmesan, for garnish

WATERCRESS AND ENDIVE
WITH AVOCADO, MELON, AND TOASTED HAZELNUTS

Some of the most interesting salads are full of as many textures as flavors. That's the heart of this refreshing winner, with the snap of endive, the elegant, rich smoothness of avocado, and the crunch of flavorful hazelnuts all joining forces to keep your teeth as happy as your tongue. You'll find the collision of the endive's mild bitterness and watermelon's over-the-top sweetness to be beyond tempting—and you might want to save a serving for seconds.

SERVES 4

1 large bunch watercress, trimmed, coarsely chopped

1 head endive, sliced crosswise

1 avocado, peeled, pitted, and diced

½ cup toasted, peeled hazelnuts, coarsely chopped

2 tablespoons extra-virgin olive oil

2 teaspoons fresh lemon juice

½ teaspoon honey

Salt and freshly ground black pepper, to taste

3 cups cubed watermelon (or substitute honeydew or cantaloupe)

1. In a large salad bowl, combine the watercress and endive. Scatter the avocado over the greens.

2. In the bowl of a food processor, pulse the hazelnuts (reserving a tablespoon) until finely ground. Add the olive oil, lemon juice, honey, salt, and pepper. Pulse until thick and smooth.

3. Drizzle half of the dressing over the greens and avocado. Season with additional salt and pepper as needed, and toss to coat. Scatter the melon cubes over the salad and drizzle the remaining dressing over top. Garnish the salad with the remaining hazelnuts and serve immediately.

NUTRITIONAL INFORMATION Per Serving: 300 cal., 24 g fat, 3 g sat. fat, 19 g carb., 6 g protein, 197 mg sodium, 9 g sugar, 8 g fiber.

Watercress and Endive
with Avocado, Melon, and
Toasted Hazelnuts

Protein-Packed
Turkey Burger

PROTEIN-PACKED TURKEY BURGER

The ideal recipe deftly satisfies hunger cravings for hours, offers a big wallop of healthy protein coupled with acceptably low amounts of fat, and skimps on the carbs. All that makes this one ideal dish for lunch, dinner, a big snack, or a meal on the go. In addition to all the straightforward health benefits, this burger delivers a truckload of savory flavor. Even if you're a diehard fan of the more traditional beef burger, the rich, interesting taste of this turkey version ensures you won't be missing a thing (especially all those beefy saturated fats!).

1. Combine the turkey, pepper, salt, garlic, scallion, and Worcestershire sauce in the canister of a blender or food processor. Pulse until chopped into a uniform texture.

2. Transfer the mix to a bowl, and fold with a spatula. Use your hands to form three patties.

3. Heat the olive oil in a large pan over medium-high heat. Lightly sear each patty, ensuring the internal temperature reaches 165 degrees F. To retain the juiciness, don't move or pierce the patties while cooking.

4. Serve each patty on a bun, with a slice of tomato and a lettuce leaf.

NUTRITIONAL INFORMATION Per Serving: 180 cal., 17 g fat, 2 g sat. fat, 30 g carb., 8 g protein, 438 mg sodium, 7 g sugar, 4 g fiber.

SERVES 3

1 pound turkey breast, diced

¼ teaspoon freshly ground black pepper

¼ teaspoon salt

1 teaspoon minced garlic

1 ounce diced scallion

1 teaspoon Worcestershire sauce

1 tablespoon olive oil

3 whole-wheat buns

3 slices tomato

3 leaves lettuce

EVENING RECIPES

4

Finishing the Day Strong

Mediterranean Cod

Steamed Cod with Fennel and Green Beans

Old-School Barbecue Chicken

Chicken and Mushroom Stroganoff

Turkey and Three-Bean Chili

Grilled Fish Tacos with Tropical Salsa

Turkey Meatballs Marinara

Crispy Almond-Baked Tilapia

Spiced Seared Tuna with Snow Pea "Slaw"

Spicy Lemon Shrimp and Herb Penne

Whole-Wheat Spaghetti with Edamame Pesto

Mussels with Tarragon and White Wine

Grilled Garlic-Lemon Sea Bass

Spicy Ricotta-and-Zucchini-Stuffed Baked Shells

Herbed Goat Cheese–Stuffed Chicken Breasts

Mexican Chicken Burgers

Squash, Tomato, and Feta Tart

Zucchini Boats with Minted Couscous

Italian Dinner Frittata

Flank Steak with Red Pepper Pesto

Green Chile Chicken Enchiladas

Beef Tenderloin with Creamy Spinach

Sirloin Steak with Peppers and Onions

Vegetable Tostadas

Bone-hugging Chili

Tristé's Quick Sloppy Joes

Eggplant and Asparagus Rollatini

Dr. Ian's Sweet Barbecue Steaks

Creole Trout Fillets with Collard Greens

Ma's Easy Eggplant Parmesan

Artichoke and Swiss Cheese–Stuffed Pork Chops

Chicken, Roasted Pepper, and Spinach Quesadillas

Grilled Barbecue Chicken and Red Onion Pizza

Chicken and Mushrooms

Pretzel-Crusted Fish Sticks with Easy Coleslaw

Roasted Turkey Sausages with Smashed German Potatoes

The way our busy days are arranged, an evening meal may be the only time that we have to spend with loved ones at the table. Despite the traditional big family dinner, big is not what you need when it comes to having a fulfilling meal. If you've eaten and snacked all day, your body will not be asking for a huge influx of calories. Eating too many calories right before going to sleep can be one of the quickest ways to gain weight. Make sure you're eating your dinner at least 2 hours before bedtime; if you get hungry a little later, then venture into the snack section (see chapter 6, page 265) and find a treat there.

As with all the recipes in this book, you don't have to worry about the calories. I have done all that for you. Simply pay attention to the ingredients, their quantity, and how you assemble them. And remember, flipping meals in the SHRED lifestyle is completely acceptable. If you want to make these recipes for an earlier meal, go right ahead. These recipes are full of nutrients and flavor and great color. Go ahead and indulge without remorse!

DANA'S FAVORITE SAVORY CHICKEN SCALOPPINI

My brother is not much of a cook, but this recipe is one that deeply pleasures him. A healthy marathon runner, he eats for peak performance, but he also likes to enjoy a good meal. Recipes like this are why the Italians (and everyone else) revere their cuisine. Although veal is traditional, the chicken in this version comes into its own when dressed in a delectable wine-and-caper sauce. The idea behind a scaloppini sauce always is to mimic the flavor of the meat in the sauce, something the addition of chicken broth in this recipe does nicely. The sauce also ensures that the thin cutlets don't dry out during cooking.

SERVES 4

Four 6-ounce skinless, boneless chicken-breast halves

¼ teaspoon salt

¼ teaspoon black pepper

2 teaspoons fresh lemon juice

¼ teaspoon chopped fresh flat-leaf parsley

¼ cup Italian-seasoned breadcrumbs

Cooking spray

1 tablespoon olive oil

1 clove garlic, minced

⅓ cup fat-free, low-sodium chicken broth

¼ cup dry white wine

1 tablespoon unsalted butter

3 tablespoons capers

1. Place each chicken breast half between 2 sheets of waxed paper and pound them to ¼-inch thick, using a rolling pin or wooden mallet. Season the breasts with salt and pepper.

2. Sprinkle the lemon juice over the chicken and dust with the parsley.

3. Place the breadcrumbs in a shallow dish. Dredge each chicken breast until coated on both sides. Lightly shake to remove excess breadcrumbs, and transfer the chicken to a clean plate.

4. Coat a large skillet with cooking spray and heat it over medium-high heat. Cook the chicken for about 5 minutes on each side, or until it is cooked through. Transfer to a plate, cover, and keep warm.

5. Add the olive oil and garlic to the pan, and sauté until the garlic begins to brown. Add the broth and wine, and cook for 1 minute, stirring constantly. Remove the pan from the heat and whisk in the butter, until the sauce is smooth. Add the capers.

6. Return the chicken to the pan. Simmer for 2 to 3 minutes and serve hot.

NUTRITIONAL INFORMATION Per Serving: 243 cal., 11 g fat, 4 g sat. fat, 6 g carb., 26 g protein, 472 mg sodium, 1 g sugar, 0 g fiber.

CHEESE-PACKED CHICKEN BREASTS

This recipe delivers a hunger-destroying dinner in a jiffy. Baking the breaded cutlet means no oil, which translates to less fat and fewer nasty free radicals. Your family isn't likely to notice the difference, though, thanks to the heavenly combination of a crunchy crust and salty melted cheese in every bite. The dish uses a nifty trick that saves calories and cholesterol, one that you can recycle for just about any breaded dish—substitute egg whites instead of whole eggs!

SERVES 4

Four 6-ounce skinless, boneless chicken-breast halves

Salt and pepper, to taste

4 slices thin-sliced provolone

½ cup all-purpose flour

¾ cup breadcrumbs, crushed

2 tablespoons chopped flat-leaf parsley

2 egg whites, beaten

1. Preheat the oven to 375 degrees F.

2. Sandwich the chicken breasts between 2 layers of waxed paper. Pound them with a mallet or heavy pan until each is about ¾-inch thick. Season each breast with salt and pepper.

3. Cut a pocket in each chicken breast half. Insert a slice of cheese into each.

4. In a shallow medium bowl, combine the flour, breadcrumbs, and parsley. Place the egg whites in a separate bowl.

5. Dip each breast in the egg, allowing any extra to drip into the bowl. Dredge in the flour mixture, and shake off any extra. Place the breasts on a baking sheet and bake for 20 to 25 minutes, or until cooked through and the internal temperature is at least 160 degrees F.

NUTRITIONAL INFORMATION Per Serving: 324 cal., 8 g fat, 3 g sat. fat, 26 g carb., 34 g protein, 293 mg sodium, 1 g sugar, 1 g fiber.

SUPER PROTEIN SALMON BURGERS

If you've never had a salmon burger, you've missed out. This heartiest of fish makes an ideal burger not just because the flavor of the fish can hold its own against beef but also because it delivers all that flavor with a whole lot less cholesterol to worry about. This particular formula makes a moist patty that's ripe with citrus zip and a few other fresh flavors. The simple mixture allows the fish's naturally wholesome taste to shine through. Although the whole-wheat buns are a nice stage for this star performer, the patties would be just as good served on their own with a nice little side salad.

1. Combine the salmon, parsley, breadcrumbs, onion, garlic, salt and pepper, and lime juice in the canister of a blender. Blend on high for 2 minutes, scraping down the sides of the blender as necessary.

2. Remove the mixture and form 4 equal patties.

3. Heat the olive oil in a large sauté pan over medium-high heat. Sear the patties for about 4 minutes each side, or until the outside is seared and the patties are cooked to medium doneness (or to desired doneness).

4. Transfer the patties to a clean plate. Toast the buns top-side down in the pan. Serve each patty on a warm, toasted bun.

NUTRITIONAL INFORMATION Per Serving: 389 cal., 29 g fat, 4 g sat. fat, 28 g carb., 31 g protein, 347 mg sodium, 4 g sugar, 3 g fiber.

SERVES 4

1 pound salmon, coarsely diced

¼ cup chopped fresh flat-leaf parsley

3 tablespoons breadcrumbs

1½ tablespoons finely diced red onion

2 cloves garlic, minced

¼ teaspoon salt

¼ teaspoon freshly ground black pepper

1 tablespoon fresh lime juice

2 tablespoons extra-virgin olive oil

4 whole-wheat buns

Grapefruit-Honey
Glazed Salmon

GRAPEFRUIT-HONEY GLAZED SALMON

This is an ideal simple and satisfying weeknight meal. You won't spend much time in the kitchen, and the result will be well worth the effort. The recipe accents salmon's rich flavor with citrus and a bit of mustardy sharpness. A tiny amount of honey offers natural sweetness that is the perfect counterpoint to the acidity of the glaze, without adding much actual sugar. It's a balance that will leave you full, without feeling heavy.

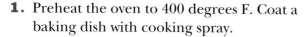

1. Preheat the oven to 400 degrees F. Coat a baking dish with cooking spray.

2. Place the salmon in the baking dish and season with salt and pepper.

3. In a small bowl, whisk together the honey, grapefruit juice and zest, olive oil, and mustard until thick and emulsified. With a pastry brush, brush the glaze on the exposed salmon and drizzle any extra over the fish.

4. Bake until the salmon is flaky and just barely pink in the center, 10 to 12 minutes. Serve warm.

NUTRITIONAL INFORMATION Per Serving: 325 cal., 15 g fat, 2 g sat. fat, 1 g carb., 44 g protein, 110 mg sodium, 1 g sugar, 0 g fiber.

SERVES 4

Cooking spray

Four 6-ounce boneless salmon fillets, preferably wild

Salt and freshly ground black pepper, to taste

1 tablespoon honey

1 tablespoon fresh grapefruit juice

½ teaspoon finely grated grapefruit zest

1 teaspoon extra-virgin olive oil

½ teaspoon Dijon mustard

CHICKEN, MUSHROOM, AND SHALLOT STIR-FRY

It's hard to beat stir-frying as a way to whip up a delicious, healthy meal in minutes. Cooking vegetables and chicken very fast at high heat seals in moisture, preserves flavor, and captures essential nutrients. Although everyone at the table will be wowed with the simple and sturdy flavors in this dish, the mix of tender and crispy textures is sure to add interest on the tongue—all in a low-fat, one-pan, scrumptious meal.

SERVES 4

3 teaspoons canola oil

3 large shallots, sliced lengthwise

6 ounces cremini mushrooms, quartered

6 ounces shiitake mushrooms, sliced

2 large cloves garlic, chopped

1 teaspoon peeled and finely chopped fresh ginger

12 ounces chicken tenders, cut into 1-inch pieces

2 teaspoons low-sodium soy sauce

1 teaspoon rice vinegar

½ teaspoon toasted sesame oil

1 teaspoon cornstarch

4 scallions, chopped

1. Heat 1 teaspoon of the canola oil in a wok or large nonstick skillet over medium-high heat. Swirl the pan until the oil is very hot. Add the shallots and mushrooms and stir-fry, stirring constantly, until the shallots are softened and the mushrooms release their liquid and begin to brown (6–8 minutes). Add the garlic and ginger and cook, stirring, for about 2 minutes more. Transfer the vegetables to a bowl and set aside.

2. Add the remaining 2 teaspoons of the canola oil to the wok and heat. Add the chicken and stir-fry until cooked and no pink remains, about 5 minutes. Return the mushroom mixture to the wok and stir to combine.

3. In a small bowl, combine the soy sauce, rice vinegar, sesame oil, and cornstarch and stir until smooth. Pour this mixture into the wok and cook, stirring, until

the liquid begins to bubble and thicken. It should glaze the chicken and vegetables.

4. Add the scallions and toss several times. Remove to a serving bowl and serve immediately.

NUTRITIONAL INFORMATION Per Serving: 186 cal., 6 g fat, 0 g sat. fat, 12 g carb., 19 g protein, 262 mg sodium, 2 g sugar, 2 g fiber.

SAVORY SUCCULENT SALMON

The hearty nature of salmon means that the fish holds up well against both sweet and savory flavors. Good thing, because both are represented in abundance here. The mix of sweet, salty, and tart makes for an intriguing palate teaser. But more important, those flavors come at very little cost in terms of unnecessary calories, fat, or other less-than-healthy additions. In fact, the fish itself delivers super good-for-you Omega-3 oils as well as a cornucopia of other essential nutrients. You can feel free to indulge in this taste sensation without risking an iota of guilt.

SERVES 4

1 tablespoon unsalted butter, melted

1 tablespoon canola oil

1 tablespoon Worcestershire sauce

1 teaspoon dried basil

1½ tablespoons brown sugar

2 tablespoons honey mustard

1 tablespoon garlic powder

¼ teaspoon salt

Four 6-ounce salmon fillets

1 lemon, cut into wedges

1. In a large bowl, combine the melted butter, canola oil, Worcestershire sauce, basil, brown sugar, mustard, garlic powder and salt. Whisk until thoroughly incorporated. Set aside 3 tablespoons of this marinade for basting.

2. Place salmon in a shallow dish and add the marinade so that each fillet is completely covered. Cover and chill for 25 to 30 minutes.

3. Preheat the broiler. Set the oven rack about 6 inches from the heat source.

4. Place the salmon on a baking sheet and broil for 10 to 12 minutes (or to desired doneness). Halfway through, brush the fish with the reserved marinade. Serve warm, and garnish each fillet with a lemon wedge.

NUTRITIONAL INFORMATION Per Serving: 292 cal., 12 g fat, 2 g sat. fat, 12 g carb., 37 g protein, 347 mg sodium, 6 g sugar, 2 g fiber.

CURRIED TURKEY SKEWERS

Sometimes simple can be amazingly satisfying. By borrowing the seasonings from Middle and East Asian cuisines, this dish paints zesty flavor over a canvas of normally mild turkey meat. Don't worry if you're not a big fan of spicy cooking—the curry in this dish is on the tame side.

1. In a medium bowl, combine the turkey, yogurt, garlic, curry, and lime juice. Stir well to combine and thoroughly coat the turkey. Let stand for 15 minutes (but no longer than 30). Meanwhile, soak twelve 8-inch skewers in water.

2. Preheat the broiler and position the rack about 8 inches from the heat. Spray a broiler pan with cooking spray.

3. Thread a turkey strip on each skewer, scraping any excess yogurt off into the bowl. Season the skewers lightly with salt and pepper and arrange them all in the same direction on the broiler pan. Cover the exposed wood of the skewers with aluminum foil.

4. Broil the skewers, turning once and re-covering the exposed wood, until the turkey is cooked through and beginning to brown (3–4 minutes per side).

5. Serve 3 skewers per portion over a bed of rice, or on greens dressed with lemon juice.

NUTRITIONAL INFORMATION Per Serving (includes 1 serving of cooked rice): 253 cal., 2 g fat, 0 g sat. fat, 24 g carb., 32 g protein, 245 mg sodium, 0 g sugar, 1 g fiber.

SERVES 4

1 pound turkey breast cutlets, cut into 12 thin strips

¼ cup nonfat Greek yogurt

2 cloves garlic, crushed

1 teaspoon mild yellow curry powder

Juice of ½ lime

Cooking spray

Salt and freshly ground black pepper, to taste

2 cups cooked white rice, for serving (or substitute greens)

MEDITERRANEAN TURKEY BURGERS

Don't be surprised if you find yourself replacing your regular beef patties with these super-moist alternatives for your next cookout. These burgers chintz on the fat but not the flavor, thanks to a wealth of herbs. Instead of buns, the burgers are captured, in true Mediterranean style, on pita bread.

SERVES 4

1 pound ground lean turkey meat

1 large shallot, minced

Salt and freshly ground black pepper, to taste

1 large egg

1 teaspoon dried oregano

½ teaspoon dried thyme

½ teaspoon garlic powder

2 ounces crumbled feta cheese

1 tablespoon extra-virgin olive oil

¼ cup nonfat Greek yogurt

Zest of ½ lemon

2 large whole-wheat sandwich pitas, halved and split

4 leaves green leaf lettuce

4 slices beefsteak tomato

1 small cucumber, sliced

1. Combine the turkey and shallots in a mixing bowl and season with salt and pepper as needed. In a small bowl, beat together the egg, oregano, thyme, and garlic powder. Pour this mixture over the turkey.

2. Add the cheese and, using your hands, mix the ingredients until well combined. Form the meat into 4 oblong patties about ½-inch thick.

3. Heat the olive oil in a large nonstick skillet over medium-high heat. Cook the burgers 5 to 6 minutes on each side, until completely cooked through.

4. While the burgers cook, combine the yogurt and lemon zest in a small bowl. Season with salt and pepper to taste. Spread 1 tablespoon of the yogurt mixture inside each pita half.

5. When the burgers are cooked, put each in a pita half. Cover with the lettuce leaf, tomato slice, and cucumber slices and serve.

NUTRITIONAL INFORMATION Per Serving: 332 cal., 14 g fat, 4 g sat. fat, 23 g carb., 29 g protein, 352 mg sodium, 3 g sugar, 3 g fiber.

Mediterranean
Turkey Burgers

TURKEY PICCATA

This low-cal version of the traditional flavor- and fat-rich piccata features the same buttery decadence that made the original such an Italian-restaurant classic. A burst of fresh lemon cuts the richness a bit and, along with salty capers, ensures that the richness isn't overwhelming. Serve it with whole-grain pasta or your favorite brown rice for a well-rounded, robust one-plate meal that will take care of even a big appetite without adding to the waistline.

SERVES 4

½ cup rice flour

Salt and freshly ground black pepper, to taste

1 pound turkey cutlets

1 tablespoon extra-virgin olive oil

1 teaspoon unsalted butter

Zest of ½ lemon

Juice of 1 lemon

½ cup low-sodium chicken stock

1 tablespoon brined capers, drained

2 tablespoons chopped fresh flat-leaf parsley

1. Spread the rice flour on a shallow plate and season well with salt and pepper. Dredge the turkey cutlets in the flour, until they are entirely coated. Shake off any excess flour. Transfer the cutlets to a clean plate.

2. Heat the olive oil and butter in a large skillet over medium heat. Add the cutlets one at a time, being careful not to overcrowd the skillet. Cook the turkey until the underside turns light golden brown, 4 to 5 minutes.

3. Flip the cutlets and cook until golden and the turkey is completely cooked through, 4 to 5 minutes more. Transfer to a plate and cover to keep warm.

4. Add the lemon zest and juice, chicken stock, and capers to the skillet and bring the liquid to a simmer, scraping up any browned bits in the pan. Cook until the liquid has reduced and thickened, 3 to 4 minutes.

5. Return the turkey to the pan and turn it a few times to coat in the sauce. Spoon excess sauce from the pan over the top. Sprinkle with parsley and serve.

NUTRITIONAL INFORMATION Per Serving (including whole-grain pasta): 251 cal., 7 g fat, 1 g sat. fat, 16 g carb., 30 g protein, 310 mg sodium, 0 g sugar, 1 g fiber.

CANNELLINI-KALE STEW

Kale is an amazing superfood, chock-full of essential vitamins, minerals, and nutrients. Nutritional value aside, this particular leafy green is at its best when partnered with white beans. The combination of creamy cannellini beans and sturdy pieces of kale in this dish calls for only a scattering of herbs and a few basic veggies to create the ultimate comfort food. You might make it the first time for the nutritional fireworks, but you'll turn to it again and again for its hearty, soul-satisfying goodness.

SERVES 4 (MAKES ABOUT 8 CUPS)

1 tablespoon extra-virgin olive oil

1 large yellow onion, chopped

2 carrots, peeled and diced

2 stalks celery, sliced

3 cloves garlic, chopped

¼ cup all-purpose flour

1 small bay leaf

1 small sprig fresh rosemary

1 sprig fresh thyme

1 quart low-sodium vegetable broth

1 bunch kale, stems removed and leaves thinly sliced

One 14-ounce can cannellini beans, drained

Freshly ground black pepper, to taste

Hot sauce, to taste, if desired

1. Heat the olive oil in a large saucepan over medium heat. Add the onion, carrots, and celery and cook, stirring occasionally, until softened, 6 to 8 minutes.

2. Add the garlic. Sprinkle the flour evenly over the vegetables and cook, stirring, until the flour is dissolved and no lumps remain, 2 to 3 minutes.

3. Add the bay leaf, rosemary, thyme, and vegetable broth. Bring to a simmer. Add the kale and cook until the kale is bright green and softened, about 5 minutes. Add the beans. Season with pepper to taste. Simmer for 8 to 10 minutes.

4. To serve, remove the rosemary, thyme, and bay leaf and discard. Ladle the stew into bowls and serve with hot sauce on the side.

NUTRITIONAL INFORMATION Per Serving: 239 cal., 5 g fat, 1 g sat. fat, 40 g carb., 8 g protein, 448 mg sodium, 2 g sugar, 8 g fiber.

OVEN-ROASTED CAJUN SNAPPER

You won't spend a lot of time preparing this Mardi Gras special, but it will seem like you did. Snapper has a naturally hearty flavor for a white fish, one that is perfectly complemented by the distinctive Cajun spice blend that you should be able to find in just about any store that sells a wide selection of spices—even outside of New Orleans. You don't need much else for your own Bourbon Street flavor parade.

1. Preheat the oven to 425 degrees F. Lightly oil a baking dish.

2. Line the baking dish with lemon slices. Brush the fish with olive oil and sprinkle a thin, even layer of Cajun spice over each fillet. Season the fish with salt and pepper and place the fish skin-side down directly on the lemon slices in the baking dish.

3. Top each fillet with a pat of butter. Bake until the fish flakes easily and is cooked through, 10 to 12 minutes. Serve warm with rice or greens.

NUTRITIONAL INFORMATION Per Serving: 287 cal., 4 g fat, 1 g sat. fat, 14 g carb., 47 g protein, 296 mg sodium, 0 g sugar, 1 g fiber.

SERVES 4

Extra-virgin olive oil, as needed

2 lemons, very thinly sliced and seeded

Four 6-ounce boneless snapper fillets, skin on

1 tablespoon Cajun spice blend

Salt and freshly ground black pepper, to taste

1 tablespoon unsalted butter, diced

2 cups cooked white rice (or substitute greens)

Braised Chicken
Thighs with Leeks

BRAISED CHICKEN THIGHS WITH LEEKS

Chicken thighs are the butcher's treasure. Although breasts are much more popular (and more expensive), thighs are more flavorful and succulent, ripe with healthy oils that keep the meat moist no matter how you cook it. The richness of the meat is perfectly cut with a sharper flavor like the leeks in this dish. Braising the chicken makes for a fork-tender delicacy that goes perfectly with simple rice or potatoes.

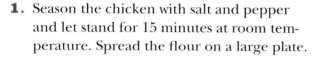

1. Season the chicken with salt and pepper and let stand for 15 minutes at room temperature. Spread the flour on a large plate.

2. Heat the olive oil in a medium nonstick skillet over medium-high heat. Dredge the chicken in flour, coating thoroughly and shaking of any excess. Cook until golden brown, turning once, about 4 minutes per side. Do not crowd the skillet. Transfer the cooked chicken to a clean plate.

3. Add the leeks and garlic to the skillet and cook, stirring, until softened, about 4 minutes. Add the thyme and chicken stock and bring the liquid to a simmer. Scrape any browned bits in the pan up with a wooden spoon.

4. Nestle the chicken into the liquid. Season the sauce with salt and pepper as needed. Cover the pan and reduce the heat to low. Cook, covered, until the chicken is fork-tender, 25 to 30 minutes.

SERVES 4

4 skinless, bone-in chicken thighs (about 1 pound large)

Salt and freshly ground black pepper, to taste

¼ cup all-purpose flour

2 tablespoons extra-virgin olive oil

3 leeks, white part only, halved lengthwise, sliced, and rinsed

2 cloves garlic, chopped

½ teaspoon dried thyme

2 cups low-sodium chicken stock

½ lemon

¼ cup chopped flat-leaf parsley

2 cups cooked rice, for serving

Continued

5. Remove the lid from the pan and simmer a few minutes to thicken and reduce the sauce. Squeeze lemon juice over the chicken and leeks. Stir gently and remove from the heat. Sprinkle the parsley over the top, and serve with the rice.

NUTRITIONAL INFORMATION Per Serving (includes 1/2 cup rice): 352 cal., 10 g fat, 2 g sat. fat, 39 g carb., 21 g protein, 277 mg sodium, 0 g sugar, 2 g fiber.

SOY SWEET-AND-SIMPLE GRILLED HALIBUT

Halibut is a delicious bit of insurance against heart disease and stroke. The Omega-3 oils and other nutrients in this white fish aid in vascular health, boost the immune system, and provide a host of other benefits—all in a low-cholesterol package. The fish is best served with a sweet-and-tangy glaze that serves as a counterpoint to the simple, fresh flavor of the fish itself. This particular glaze is so good that it's likely to sway the nonfish eaters in your house. If not, the glaze is just as good on lean pork cuts such as pork loin.

1. Preheat the grill over medium-high heat (or heat the broiler).

2. In a small bowl, whisk together the maple syrup, butter, lemon juice, tamari, garlic, and pepper until completely combined. Set aside.

3. Using long-handled tongs and a paper towel moistened with canola oil, lightly coat the grill.

4. Brush the halibut with the glaze. Grill for about 4 minutes on each side, regularly brushing the fish with more glaze. Cook until the fish flakes easily with fork.

NUTRITIONAL INFORMATION Per Serving: 396 cal., 13 g fat, 5 g sat. fat, 7 g carb., 60 g protein, 314 mg sodium, 7 g sugar, 0 g fiber.

SERVES 2

1 tablespoon pure maple syrup

1 tablespoon unsalted butter, melted

½ tablespoon lemon juice

1 teaspoon tamari sauce

½ teaspoon minced garlic

¼ teaspoon pepper

Canola oil, as needed

2 halibut steaks

CHICKEN BREASTS WITH CARAMELIZED PEARS AND SHALLOTS

There is no better way to dress up plain chicken breasts than with caramelized fruit. Caramelizing ingredients such as the pears in this recipe draws out and accentuates their natural sugars, adding sweetness without adding refined sweeteners. The other savory flavors round out the dish, countering the sweetness with a touch of tart and creating an enticing combination that brings a whole new level of excitement to this healthy white-meat standard.

SERVES 4

Cooking spray

Four 6-ounce skinless, boneless chicken breasts

Salt and freshly ground black pepper, to taste

2 tablespoons extra-virgin olive oil

3 large shallots, peeled and sliced lengthwise

1 tablespoon cider vinegar

2 ripe but firm pears, peeled, cored and thickly sliced (recommend Bosc or Anjou)

2 teaspoons honey

Pinch dried thyme

1. Preheat the oven to 375 degrees F. Coat a baking dish with cooking spray.

2. Season the chicken on both sides with salt and pepper. Heat the olive oil in a large nonstick skillet over medium-high heat. Cook the chicken, turning once, until golden brown, 4 to 5 minutes per side.

3. Transfer the chicken to the baking dish and cover the dish with aluminum foil. Bake until the chicken is cooked through, about 20 minutes. Remove from the oven and keep warm.

4. While the chicken cooks, heat the skillet you used for the chicken over medium heat. Add the shallots and cook, stirring occasionally, until they begin to brown, 5 to 6 minutes.

Continued

Chicken Breasts with
Caramelized Pears
and Shallots

5. Add the vinegar and use a wooden spoon to scrape up any browned bits in the pan. Add the pears, honey, and thyme. Season with salt and pepper to taste. Cook, stirring frequently, until the liquid evaporates and the pears begin to brown on the edges (soft but not falling apart), about 5 minutes.

6. Slice the cooked chicken crosswise on the diagonal. Divide among 4 plates and spoon the caramelized pears and shallots over the top. Serve warm.

NUTRITIONAL INFORMATION Per Serving: 272 cal., 9 g fat, 1 g sat. fat, 16 g carb., 30 g protein, 241 mg sodium, 9 g sugar, 2 g fiber.

TILAPIA À L'ORANGE

This dish has a fancy name that's just another way of saying "super delicious, super inexpensive white fish saturated with an eye-popping combination of flavors." There are different types of sweetness in the culinary world, and the unique marinade in this recipe makes great use of clean fresh citrus tones and the natural goodness of honey. But you'll also find notes of ginger, silky tartness, and sharp saltiness—all of which transform a simple fish into something much, much more. Make extra of the marinade and refrigerate it for later. It works magic with chicken breasts.

1. Preheat the oven to 375 degrees F. Coat a 9 x 13–inch baking dish with cooking spray.

2. In a large bowl, whisk together the orange juice, tamari, honey, garlic, ginger, and vinegar. Submerge the fish in the marinade, cover, and refrigerate for 30 minutes to 1 hour.

3. Remove the tilapia from the marinade, letting any excess run off. Lay the fish in the baking dish and discard the marinade.

4. Bake, turning the fish every 10 minutes, until it flakes easily with a fork, about 40 minutes.

NUTRITIONAL INFORMATION Per Serving: 219 cal., 0 g fat, 0 g sat. fat, 13 g carb., 37 g protein, 327 mg sodium, 12 g sugar, 0 g fiber.

SERVES 4

Cooking spray

½ cup fresh orange juice

1 tablespoon tamari sauce

2 tablespoons honey

1 clove garlic, finely minced

½ teaspoon grated fresh ginger

2 tablespoons balsamic vinegar

Four 6-ounce tilapia fillets, rinsed and patted dry

Shrimp Fried
Brown Rice

SHRIMP FRIED BROWN RICE

Here's a way to have the pleasure of Chinese takeout without all the unhealthy additives. The key to keeping this dish light, lively, and flavorful is quick cooking in a wok over high heat. The process seals in nutrients and makes sure more delicate additions like delicious snow peas stay crisp and green. Traditional Asian elements like rice vinegar and ginger ensure that the finished dish tastes boldly authentic without ramping up fats or calories.

1. In a small bowl, combine the soy sauce, vinegar, and sesame oil and stir to thoroughly mix. Set aside.

2. Heat the canola oil in a wok or large skillet over high heat until very hot. Add the carrot and cook, stirring constantly, for 1 minute. Add the garlic, ginger, and shrimp and stir-fry until the shrimp is cooked halfway through, about 2 minutes. Add the snow peas and rice and cook, stirring, for about 1 minute. Pour the soy sauce mixture into the pan and stir well to combine.

3. Drizzle the beaten egg over the rice in the pan and continue stirring aggressively until the egg is completely cooked and speckled in the rice.

4. Remove from the heat and transfer to a serving bowl. Scatter the scallions over the top and serve hot.

NUTRITIONAL INFORMATION Per Serving: 202 cal., 4 g fat, 0 g sat. fat, 29 g carb., 11 g protein, 232 mg sodium, 1 g sugar.

SERVES 4

1 tablespoon low-sodium soy sauce

2 teaspoons rice vinegar

1 teaspoon toasted sesame oil

1 tablespoon canola oil

1 carrot, peeled and diced

2 cloves garlic, minced

2 teaspoons finely chopped, peeled, fresh ginger

8 ounces medium shrimp, peeled, deveined, and chopped

4 ounces snow peas, thinly sliced lengthwise

2 cups cooked brown rice

1 large egg, beaten

4 scallions, sliced

SEARED MUSTARD PORK CHOPS
WITH CIDER-BRAISED ONIONS

Pork chops have an appealingly delicate flavor, but if you really want to hit the ball out of the park at dinnertime, you have to coat them in a scintillating spice rub. Not only do the spices in this dish add a symphony of complex flavors to the meat, the rub itself forms a thin crust that seals in moisture so that the meat doesn't dry out during cooking. You can even use it on chicken or white fish!

SERVES 4

2 teaspoons unsalted butter

1 large white onion, sliced into ¼-inch rings (rings kept intact)

3 cloves garlic, smashed

Salt and freshly ground black pepper, to taste

¼ teaspoon dried thyme

1 tablespoon cider vinegar

1 cup apple cider

4 small boneless pork chops, about ½-inch thick

2 tablespoons all-purpose flour

1 teaspoon mustard powder

½ teaspoon sweet paprika

1 tablespoon extra-virgin olive oil

1. Melt the butter in a large skillet over medium heat. Add the onion slices in a single layer. Add the garlic, salt, pepper, and thyme. Cook, undisturbed, until the onion begins to brown on the bottom, 6 to 8 minutes.

2. Add the vinegar without moving the onion and cook for about 1 minute. Add the cider and bring to a simmer. Reduce the heat to low and cover.

3. While the onion cooks, season the pork chops with salt and pepper. In a shallow plate, combine the flour, mustard, and paprika. Dredge the chops on both sides and shake off any excess.

4. Heat the olive oil in a medium skillet over medium-high heat. Cook the pork chops until golden, 3 to 4 minutes per side.

5. Remove the lid from the onion, increase the heat to medium, and rest the pork chops directly on top of the onion slices in the pan. Cover and cook until the chops

are completely cooked through, 6 to 8 minutes.

6. Transfer the chops to a serving platter, and spoon the cooked onion over the top. Cover with a tent made of aluminum foil to keep the chops warm. Raise the heat under the pan to medium-high and simmer the liquid in the pan until thickened, about 5 minutes. Pour the sauce over the chops and serve.

NUTRITIONAL INFORMATION Per Serving: 386 cal., 18 g fat, 7 g sat. fat, 7 g carb., 40 g protein, 222 mg sodium, 0 g sugar, 1 g fiber.

PORK ROAST WITH CAULIFLOWER MASH

This is the perfect substitute for traditional Sunday pot roast and mashed potatoes. Light but still filling, this dish delivers all the high notes of that classic weekender meal with a fraction of the sugar and fat. The cauliflower serves as an ideal stage for a touch of lemon and the bite of pecorino. Don't worry if you have leftovers; the pork will keep, refrigerated, for almost a week and tastes great reheated.

SERVES 4

Cooking spray

For the pork:

2 shallots, roughly chopped

3 cloves garlic

1 tablespoon extra-virgin olive oil

2 sprigs fresh thyme, leaves only

¼ teaspoon salt

½ teaspoon freshly ground black pepper

½ teaspoon ground cumin

One 3-pound boneless pork loin roast

1. Preheat the oven to 350 degrees F. Coat a shallow baking dish with cooking spray.

2. In the bowl of a food processor, combine the shallots, garlic, olive oil, thyme leaves, salt, pepper, and cumin and pulse until it forms a paste.

3. Pat the pork dry with paper towels. Spread the paste evenly over the surface of the pork and transfer it to the baking dish. Add about 3 tablespoons water to the dish.

4. Roast until a meat thermometer inserted into the center of the meat registers 145 degrees F, about 1 hour (20 minutes per pound). Remove the pork from the oven, cover loosely with aluminum foil and let stand at least 10 minutes before slicing.

5. While the pork rests, make the cauliflower mash. In a large saucepan, combine the cauliflower, garlic, lemon peel, and bay

leaf. Cover with water. Bring to a boil over medium-high heat and cook until the cauliflower is very soft and meets no resistance when a knife is inserted into the stems, 15 to 20 minutes.

6. Drain in a colander and remove the lemon peel and bay leaf. Transfer the cauliflower to a large bowl. Add the olive oil and cheese, and season with pepper as needed. Mash with a potato masher until coarse and chunky but well mixed.

7. Thinly slice the pork and serve with the cauliflower mash on the side. Drizzle any pan juices from the baking dish over the pork.

PORK: NUTRITIONAL INFORMATION Per Serving: 429 cal., 26 g fat, 8 g sat. fat, 3 g carb., 71 g protein, 309 mg sodium, 0 g sugar, 0 g fiber.

CAULIFLOWER: NUTRITIONAL INFORMATION Per Serving: 143 cal., 8 g fat, 4 g sat. fat, 9 g carb., 10 g protein, 298 mg sodium, 4 g sugar, 4 g fiber.

For the cauliflower mash:

1 head cauliflower, trimmed and cut into florets

1 clove garlic, smashed

1 wide strip lemon peel

1 small bay leaf

2 tablespoons extra-virgin olive oil

⅓ cup grated pecorino

freshly ground black pepper

Asian Grilled Pork
Tenderloin with Celery
Root—Mandarin Slaw

ASIAN GRILLED PORK TENDERLOIN

WITH CELERY ROOT–MANDARIN SLAW

This dish makes good use of the East Asian philosophy of cooking with vivid spices and unique ingredients rather than relying on fat and heavier additions for tongue appeal. Rice vinegar and mandarin oranges—which are actually a type of juicy tangerine—create a dramatic balance between tart and sweet in the slaw, while the ginger and traditional Chinese spice blend bring the lean pork tenderloin to life. You won't miss the fat and extra calories.

1. Lightly oil the grill with vegetable oil. Preheat a gas grill on medium-high or prepare a medium-hot fire in a charcoal grill.

2. Pat the pork dry with paper towels. In a small bowl, combine the brown sugar, salt, five-spice powder, ginger, and pepper, stirring until combined. Rub the spice mix evenly over the pork, patting the rub down onto the surface of the meat.

3. Grill the pork, covered, turning it several times. Cook until an instant-read thermometer inserted in the thickest part registers 145 degrees F, about 20 minutes. Transfer the pork to a platter and cover with a tent made of aluminum foil. Let rest for 5 to 10 minutes before slicing.

4. While the pork is cooking, grate the celery root, using the large holes of a box grater, into a serving bowl. In a small bowl, whisk together the rice vinegar, orange zest and juice, and canola oil until thick and emulsified. Season with pepper to taste.

SERVES 4

Vegetable oil, as needed

For the pork:

1 whole pork tenderloin (about 1½ pounds)

2 teaspoons light brown sugar

⅛ teaspoon salt

1 teaspoon Chinese five-spice powder

½ teaspoon ground ginger

½ teaspoon freshly ground black pepper

Continued

For the slaw:

1 large celery root, peeled

1 teaspoon rice vinegar

Zest of ½ orange

2 teaspoons fresh orange juice

1 tablespoon canola oil

Freshly ground black pepper, to taste

One 15-ounce can mandarin oranges, drained

¼ cup slivered almonds, toasted

1 small bunch scallions, sliced

5. Pour the dressing over the celery root. Let stand about 10 minutes, tossing occasionally. Add the oranges, almonds, and scallions and toss. Season with additional pepper as needed.

6. Slice the pork crosswise on the diagonal and serve with the slaw on the side.

PORK: NUTRITIONAL INFORMATION Per Serving: 222 cal., 6 g fat, 2 g sat. fat, 2 g carb., 36 g protein, 373 mg sodium, 2 g sugar, 0 g fiber.

SLAW: NUTRITIONAL INFORMATION Per Serving: 164 cal., 5 g fat, 0 g sat. fat, 16 g carb., 4 g protein, 162 mg sodium, 10 g sugar, 4 g fiber.

POACHED LEMON-PEPPER CHICKEN BREASTS

Few flavors are as powerful and yet pleasant as concentrated citrus. The fresh tartness of lemon brings subtle, white-meat chicken to life, saturating the meat and providing a burst of flavor in every bite. The peppercorns and chili flakes keep the lemon flavor in check and provide an interesting, down-to-earth counterpoint to it. Combined, the flavor notes create the impression of a much more substantial dish, when the meal is really low-fat and healthy as can be.

1. Combine the lemons, onion, garlic, parsley, peppercorns, salt, and chili flakes in a large deep skillet. Fill the skillet with water. Bring the mixture to a boil over medium-high heat and simmer for 2 to 3 minutes.

2. Add the chicken breasts, being sure they are submerged. When the water returns to a boil, cook for about 2 minutes. Cover the pan, turn off the heat, and let the chicken stand for 20 minutes, until cooked through.

3. Remove the chicken from the pan and discard the vegetables. Slice the chicken crosswise against the grain and serve with the rice.

NUTRITIONAL INFORMATION Per Serving: 304 cal., 2 g fat, 0 g sat. fat, 33 g carb., 33 g protein, 402 mg sodium, 4 g sugar, 5 g fiber.

SERVES 4

2 lemons, sliced

1 small yellow onion, chopped

3 cloves garlic, smashed

1 small bunch flat-leaf parsley

2 teaspoons whole black peppercorns

½ teaspoon salt

½ teaspoon red chili flakes

4 large skinless, boneless chicken breasts

2 cups cooked brown rice (or substitute steamed vegetables), for serving

MEDITERRANEAN COD

The secret to an amazingly low-cal, low-fat fish dish that doesn't skimp on flavors is to leverage the exceptional fresh flavors of the Mediterranean. The preparation of this heart-healthy fish could not be simpler. But the fish really comes to life under a coat of amazing salsa, rich in garden-fresh ingredients and thick with simple, sturdy and strongly flavored herbs.

SERVES 4

Salsa

1½ cups chopped tomato

1 cup finely chopped zucchini

½ cup finely chopped roasted peppers

2 tablespoons finely chopped red onion

1 tablespoon finely chopped fresh basil

1 tablespoon finely chopped fresh flat-leaf parsley

2 teaspoons extra-virgin olive oil

2 teaspoons fresh lemon juice

1½ teaspoons capers, rinsed and drained

⅛ teaspoon black pepper

1 clove garlic, minced

Fish

Four 6-ounce cod fillets

¼ teaspoon lemon pepper

1 teaspoon olive oil

1. In a large bowl, combine all the salsa ingredients and mix well to incorporate. Cover and refrigerate.

2. Pat the cod fillets dry and season with lemon pepper. Heat olive oil in a nonstick skillet over medium-high heat.

3. Sauté the fillets for 4 minutes on each side or until the fish flakes with a fork. Do not overcook. Serve hot with salsa spooned over top.

NUTRITIONAL INFORMATION Per Serving: 206 cal., 5 g fat, 1 g sat. fat, 6 g carb., 33 g protein, 360 mg sodium, 4 g sugar, 1 g fiber.

STEAMED COD WITH FENNEL
AND GREEN BEANS

Here's a refreshing meal that won't weigh you down. Steaming the delicate fish makes sure the valuable nutrients and oils stay intact, along with the flavor. Add some simple veggies and a hint of licorice courtesy of fennel, and you have a good-for-you dinner for summer days and beyond.

1. Preheat the oven to 400 degrees F. Cut 4 large pieces of parchment paper about 14 inches long.

2. Divide the fennel and green beans into 4 bunches and place each bunch on a parchment sheet, arranging the beans so they all curve in the same direction. Season with salt and pepper.

3. Top the vegetables on each parchment sheet with a piece of cod. Press down so that the fish lies flat. Drizzle a little olive oil over each fillet and season with salt and pepper. Lay 2 slices of lemon on top of each piece of cod.

4. Fold the long ends of each parchment sheet over the fish and fold the edges together in ½-inch creases. Continue folding with all the packets. Fold the opposite ends under the fish like a package.

5. Place the packets on a baking sheet and bake for 20 minutes. To serve, put each packet on a plate. Cut the paper open and sprinkle the reserved fennel fronds over the top.

NUTRITIONAL INFORMATION Per Serving: 202 cal., 5 g fat, 1 g sat. fat, 7 g carb., 31 g protein, 307 mg sodium, 0 g sugar, 4 g fiber.

SERVES 4

1 small bulb fennel, trimmed, fronds removed and reserved, bulb sliced through the core into thin wedges

6 ounces baby green beans, trimmed

Salt and freshly ground black pepper, to taste

Four 6-ounce center-cut cod fillets

Extra-virgin olive oil, as needed

8 thin slices of lemon, seeds removed

OLD-SCHOOL BARBECUE CHICKEN

I have always loved barbecue chicken. It brings back some of my favorite childhood memories of sitting in Aunt Chris's backyard watching the adults make quick work over the brick-encased grill. I offer this recipe to you because it is not only ridiculously tasty, but it develops maximum flavors with few ingredients. The trick is to use the barbecue sauce without letting it burn. A big problem when grilling chicken with barbecue sauce is that the sugar in the sauce tends to caramelize and quickly burns—leading to a less-than-perfect flavor and unhealthy char. By baking the chicken, as in this recipe, the sauce turns into a wonderful glaze on the meat.

SERVES 4

Four 6-ounce skinless, boneless chicken-breast halves

¼ teaspoon salt

⅛ teaspoon pepper

1 cup all-purpose flour

¼ cup extra-virgin olive oil

½ cup barbecue sauce

1. Preheat the oven to 375 degrees F.

2. Lightly season the chicken breasts with the salt and pepper. Add the flour to a 1-gallon resealable plastic bag. Add the chicken and shake well until it is completely coated.

3. Heat the olive oil in a large skillet over high heat. Brown the chicken on each side, cooking about 2 to 3 minutes per side.

4. Transfer the chicken to a nonstick baking sheet. Blot the top of each breast dry. Baste with barbecue sauce.

5. Bake the chicken for 10 minutes, or until the sauce is thickened on the surface of the breasts.

NUTRITIONAL INFORMATION Per Serving: 460 cal., 18 g fat, 4 g sat. fat, 40 g carb., 28 g protein, 425 mg sodium, 16 g sugar, 1 g fiber.

Old-School Barbecue Chicken

CHICKEN AND MUSHROOM STROGANOFF

This Russian creation has traveled around the world. The simple, creamy brown sauce coating tender meat strips is the perfect match to rich egg noodles that seem to melt on the tongue. Substitute chicken for the traditional beef and use a few low-fat alternatives and you wind up with this terrific dish. It cuts out a lot of the fat, sodium, and unhealthy parts of the original without sacrificing any of the decadence.

SERVES 4

1 tablespoon extra-virgin olive oil

2 large skinless, boneless chicken breasts (about 1 pound), cut into 1-inch cubes

Salt and freshly ground black pepper, to taste

1 pound cremini mushrooms, quartered

2 large shallots, sliced

2 cloves garlic, minced

½ cup dry white wine

2 tablespoons cornstarch

1 cup low-sodium chicken stock

¼ cup low-fat sour cream

¼ cup chopped fresh chives

6 ounces wide egg noodles, cooked according to package directions

1. Heat the olive oil in a large skillet over medium-high heat. Season the chicken well with salt and pepper. Sear it until browned on all sides, turning frequently, 6 to 8 minutes total. Transfer the chicken to a plate.

2. Add the mushrooms to the skillet, season them with salt and pepper, and stir frequently until softened and the edges are beginning to brown, 6 to 8 minutes. Add the shallots and garlic and cook until softened, 3 to 4 minutes.

3. Add the wine, scraping up any browned bits in the pan. Cook until the liquid is nearly evaporated.

4. In a small bowl, whisk the cornstarch into the chicken stock until smooth. Add to the skillet and bring to a simmer. Return the chicken to the pan along with any juices from the plate. Stir well, reduce the heat to a simmer, and cook for 10 minutes or until the chicken is completely cooked through.

5. Remove the pan from the heat and stir in the sour cream. Season with salt and pepper to taste. Stir in the chives and pour the sauce over the cooked egg noodles. Serve hot.

NUTRITIONAL INFORMATION Per Serving: 379 cal., 12 g fat, 2 g sat. fat, 81 g carb., 29 g protein, 250 mg sodium, 2 g sugar, 2 g fiber.

TURKEY AND THREE-BEAN CHILI

When it comes to chili, beef might be hearty, but turkey is the ultimate flavor sponge. And given the bounty of wonderful ingredients in this dinner, you won't be missing the beef flavor or fat or salt. The gusto in this version is helped along by three very different—but protein heavy—beans. Be sure to drain and rinse the beans thoroughly, because the natural canning juices can contain a lot of sugar and other by-products that you don't need.

SERVES 6 TO 8

2 tablespoons olive oil

1 pound lean ground turkey meat

1 yellow onion, chopped

3 cloves garlic, chopped

1 yellow bell pepper, stemmed, seeded, and chopped

1 small jalapeño, seeded and minced

1 tablespoon tomato paste

1 tablespoon chili powder

One 12-ounce bottle lager beer

One 14-ounce can crushed tomatoes

2 cups low-sodium chicken stock

One 15-ounce can reduced-sodium kidney beans, rinsed and drained

One 15-ounce can reduced-sodium pinto beans, rinsed and drained

1. Heat the olive oil in a large saucepan over medium heat. Add the turkey and break it up with a wooden spoon. Cook until browned, 6 to 8 minutes. Add the onion, garlic, bell pepper, and jalapeño and cook, stirring, until softened, 6 to 8 minutes.

2. Add the tomato paste and chili powder and cook, stirring, until the paste begins to caramelize, 3 to 4 minutes. Add the beer and stir to scrape up any browned bits in the bottom of the pan.

3. Bring to a simmer and cook until the liquid has reduced by half, about 5 minutes. Add the tomatoes, chicken stock, and beans. Bring to a boil.

4. Reduce the heat to a simmer, cover, and cook until very thick, 35 to 40 minutes. Season with pepper to taste.

5. In a small bowl, combine the yogurt, lime zest and juice, and cumin. Ladle the chili into bowls and top each bowl with a dollop of the lime yogurt. Garnish with the scallions and serve.

NUTRITIONAL INFORMATION Per Serving: 257 cal., 0 g fat, 0 g sat. fat, 47 g carb., 10 g protein, 424 mg sodium, 3 g sugar, 13 g fiber.

One 15-ounce can reduced-sodium cannellini beans, rinsed and drained

Freshly ground black pepper, to taste

½ cup nonfat Greek yogurt

Zest of 1 lime

Juice of ½ lime

¼ teaspoon ground cumin

Sliced scallions, for serving

Grilled Fish Tacos with
Tropical Salsa

GRILLED FISH TACOS WITH TROPICAL SALSA

Even people who don't normally like fish absolutely love these tacos. Each one explodes with fun and fresh flavors that capture a south-of-the-border magic. White fish also brings a lot of super-healthy Omega-3 oils, along with an alluring texture. The seasonal garden-fresh additions add fat-free flavor in abundance and a little extra crunch in the mix. You'll find this is a great cookout option, or just a wonderful change of pace in your weeknight dinner lineup.

1. In a medium bowl, combine the pineapple, mango, onion, jalapeño, cumin, and lime juice. Stir well, taste, and add pepper as necessary. Add the cilantro, and mix well. Refrigerate until ready to serve.

2. Preheat a gas grill on medium-high or prepare a medium-hot fire in a charcoal grill.

3. In a small bowl, combine the olive oil, garlic powder, cumin, and chili powder. Brush both sides of the fish with the spiced oil and season the fish with pepper.

4. Grill the fish, turning once, until cooked through but still moist, about 3 minutes per side (depends on the thickness). Grill the tortillas quickly on each side until grill marks just appear. Wrap them in a towel to keep warm.

SERVES 4

For the salsa:

½ cup fresh pineapple chunks, drained and finely diced

½ mango, peeled and finely diced

1 small red onion, minced

½ jalapeño pepper, seeded and minced

Pinch ground cumin

Juice of ½ lime

Freshly ground black pepper, to taste

¼ cup finely chopped fresh cilantro leaves

Continued

For the tacos:

1 tablespoon olive oil

¼ teaspoon garlic powder

¼ teaspoon ground cumin

Pinch chili powder

¾ pound fresh grouper (or other firm white fish, such as sea bass or halibut)

Freshly ground black pepper, to taste

8 small soft reduced-sodium flour tortillas

Cilantro sprigs, for serving

1 avocado, peeled, pitted, and sliced, for serving

5. Break the grilled fish into large chunks. Fill the tortillas with pieces of fish, a spoonful of salsa, 1 or 2 cilantro sprigs, and some sliced avocado. Serve warm.

NUTRITIONAL INFORMATION Per Serving: 340 cal., 14 g fat, 2 g sat. fat, 37 g carb., 25 g protein, 433 mg sodium, 11 g sugar, 6 g fiber.

TURKEY MEATBALLS MARINARA

Few dishes are as downright comforting as meatballs and spaghetti. Lean turkey allows the traditional Italian flavors to shine through. Substitute a whole-wheat pasta or long-grain wild rice to boost the fiber in this dish.

SERVES 4 TO 6
(ABOUT 24 MEATBALLS)

1 pound lean ground turkey

2 shallots, finely chopped

2 cloves garlic, minced

2 tablespoons grated parmesan

2 teaspoons Italian seasoning

Pinch cayenne pepper

Salt and freshly ground black pepper, to taste

4 saltine crackers, crushed

1 large egg, beaten

2.5 cups reduced-sugar reduced-sodium jarred marinara sauce

1 pound cooked spaghetti (or substitute your favorite pasta)

1. In a large mixing bowl, combine the turkey, shallots, garlic, parmesan, Italian seasoning, and cayenne and mix well. Season with salt and pepper, and add the cracker crumbs and egg. Use your hands to mix until well combined. Wet your hands and roll the meat mixture into 1-inch balls.

2. Pour the marinara sauce into a deep, wide, straight-sided skillet or a Dutch oven over medium heat. When it is simmering, carefully drop the meatballs into the sauce. Cover the pan.

3. After a minute or so, reduce the heat to medium-low and shake the pan gently to move the meatballs and prevent sticking. Cook until the meatballs are cooked through, 20 to 25 minutes.

4. Remove the meatballs and add the cooked spaghetti to the sauce. Stir to coat the pasta and then transfer to a serving platter. Place meatballs on top and cover with the remaining sauce and serve.

NUTRITIONAL INFORMATION Per Serving: 345 cal., 15 g fat, 4 g sat. fat, 38 g carb., 31 g protein, 477 mg sodium, 5 g sugar, 3 g fiber.

Turkey Meatballs
Marinara

CRISPY ALMOND-BAKED TILAPIA

Tilapia has become popular not only because it's inexpensive, but also because it goes so well with so many other ingredients. It can also hold its own when breaded, as in this dish. The panko breadcrumbs make for a delicate crunch in every bite of fish, and the mix of lemon and lime plays perfectly against the pleasantly mild flavor of the fish itself. Baking ensures the fish is healthier than it would be fried, without losing any of its allure.

SERVES 4

Cooking spray

4 tilapia fillets (4–6 ounces each)

Salt and pepper, to taste

⅓ cup sliced almonds, finely chopped

½ cup whole-wheat panko

Zest of ½ lemon

Zest of 1 lime

¼ cup finely chopped fresh flat-leaf parsley

2 teaspoons olive oil

1. Preheat the oven to 425 degrees F. Lightly grease a 9 x 13–inch baking dish with cooking spray.

2. Season the fish lightly with salt and pepper. In a small bowl, combine the almonds, panko, lemon and lime zests, and parsley. Drizzle the olive oil over the mixture and toss with a fork to moisten the crumbs.

3. Arrange the fish fillets in the baking dish and pack a thin layer of the breadcrumb mixture over the surface of each fillet.

4. Bake until the breadcrumbs are golden brown and fish is cooked through, 10 to 12 minutes. Serve warm.

NUTRITIONAL INFORMATION Per Serving: 242 cal., 7 g fat, 1 g sat. fat, 7 g carb., 33 g protein, 339 mg sodium, 1 g sugar, 2 g fiber.

Crispy
Almond-Baked
Tilapia

Spiced Seared Tuna with
Snow Pea "Slaw"

SPICED SEARED TUNA WITH SNOW PEA "SLAW"

Tuna delivers just about the most assertive flavor of any fish, and even more so when you bathe it in a combination of distinctive spices. Sear it well and leave it medium-rare for a stunning meal that will win over even the fish haters at your table. Snow pea slaw is the perfect accompaniment—a breeze to make, and so fantastically bright and flavorful that you might want to make extra to eat as a snack.

1. In a small bowl, combine the ginger, coriander, cumin, paprika, cayenne, salt, and pepper. Sprinkle an even layer of the spice mixture over both sides of each tuna steak. Press the mix onto the fish. Let stand while you make the slaw.

2. Stack 5 or 6 snow peas on top of each other and, using a very sharp knife, slice them lengthwise into thin strips. Repeat with the remaining snow peas and transfer them to a serving bowl.

3. In a separate bowl, combine the mayonnaise and lemon juice and stir to mix. Pour this mixture over the snow peas. Lightly season with salt and pepper and gently toss to dress.

SERVES 4

1 teaspoon ground ginger

1 teaspoon ground coriander

½ teaspoon ground cumin

½ teaspoon sweet paprika

¼ teaspoon cayenne pepper

Salt and freshly ground black pepper, to taste

4 tuna steaks (about 6 ounces each)

8 ounces snow peas

2 tablespoons low-fat mayonnaise

1 teaspoon lemon juice

1 tablespoon olive oil

Continued

4. Heat the olive oil in a cast iron skillet or nonstick skillet over medium-high heat. Add the tuna and sear, turning once, until the outer edges turn gray, about 1 minute per side for medium-rare. Remove the tuna from the pan and let stand 3 to 5 minutes.

5. To serve, slice the tuna against the grain into thin slices and serve with the slaw on the side.

NUTRITIONAL INFORMATION Per Serving: 315 cal., 12 g fat, 3 g sat. fat, 7 g carb., 42 g protein, 293 mg sodium, 3 g sugar, 2 g fiber.

SPICY LEMON SHRIMP AND HERB PENNE

The richness of shrimp lends itself to spicy dishes full of brio and exciting flavors. Don't hesitate to make extra; the dish keeps refrigerated for a week and loses nothing when reheated.

1. Bring a large pot of water to a boil over high heat and salt it generously. Cook the penne according to package instructions. Drain the pasta, reserving ½ cup of the cooking liquid.

2. While the pasta cooks, heat the olive oil in a large, deep skillet over medium-high heat. Add the shallots and garlic and stir until they are softened, 3 to 4 minutes. Add the shrimp and toss them in the pan, until they begin to turn pink.

3. Add the butter and chili flakes and toss until the butter melts and glazes the shrimp. Cook until the shrimp are cooked through, 2 to 3 minutes. Add the parsley, basil, chives, lemon zest, and lemon juice. Season with salt and pepper to taste and toss well to combine.

4. Add the cooked pasta to the skillet and toss until well combined. Add 1 or 2 table-spoons of the reserved cooking water to moisten the pasta, if needed, and toss until very hot. Transfer to a serving bowl and serve immediately.

NUTRITIONAL INFORMATION Per Serving: 537 cal., 7 g fat, 1 g sat. fat, 86 g carb., 21 g protein, 214 mg sodium, 4 g sugar, 0 g fiber.

SERVES 4

¾ pound penne pasta

½ tablespoon extra-virgin olive oil

2 shallots, chopped

2 cloves garlic, minced

9 ounces medium shrimp, peeled and deveined

1 teaspoon unsalted butter

½ teaspoon dried chili flakes

¼ cup chopped fresh flat-leaf parsley

¼ cup chopped fresh basil leaves

2 tablespoons chopped fresh chives

Zest of 1 lemon

Juice of ½ lemon

Salt and freshly ground black pepper, to taste

WHOLE-WHEAT SPAGHETTI

WITH EDAMAME PESTO

There are lots of ways to put a healthy spin on traditional Italian cooking, but this is one of the most delectable you'll encounter. Instead of the classic basil, this recipe substitutes protein-, vitamin-, and fiber-rich edamame in the pesto. Combined with a wealth of almonds and a touch of citrus, these delicious green soybeans make for a simple but stunning pasta sauce with a little more earthiness and brightness than basil provides.

SERVES 4

1 cup frozen shelled edamame, thawed

2 cloves garlic, chopped

¼ cup sliced almonds, toasted

¼ cup fresh flat-leaf parsley leaves

Zest of ½ lemon

⅓ cup finely grated parmesan, plus more for garnish

¼ cup extra-virgin olive oil, plus more as needed

Salt and freshly ground black pepper, to taste

1 pound whole-wheat spaghetti

1. Combine the edamame, garlic, and almonds in the bowl of a food processor and pulse until finely chopped. Add the parsley, lemon zest, parmesan, and olive oil and pulse until well combined and the edamame is very finely chopped. Transfer the pesto to a large mixing bowl and season with salt and pepper to taste.

2. Bring a large pot of water to a boil and salt it generously. Boil the pasta according to the instructions on the package. Just before draining, pour 2 or 3 tablespoons of the pasta cooking water into the bowl with the pesto and stir it to loosen.

3. Drain the pasta and transfer it to the pesto bowl and toss with tongs until well coated. Divide the pasta among four serving plates and serve with parmesan.

NUTRITIONAL INFORMATION Per Serving: 376 cal., 22 g fat, 4 g sat. fat, 34 g carb., 13 g protein, 317 mg sodium, 1 g sugar, 7 g fiber.

Whole-Wheat Spaghetti
with Edamame Pesto

Mussels with Tarragon
and White Wine

MUSSELS WITH TARRAGON AND WHITE WINE

The best mussels are all about delicate ocean flavors. A classic addition to cooked mussels, tarragon delivers a faintly licorice flavor that makes itself known without undermining the rich natural taste of the shellfish. Citrus and fresh herbs join forces with a little white wine to make this dish really sparkle. This dish would be right at home as the star of a special occasion dinner.

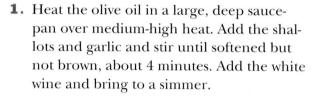

1. Heat the olive oil in a large, deep saucepan over medium-high heat. Add the shallots and garlic and stir until softened but not brown, about 4 minutes. Add the white wine and bring to a simmer.

2. Add the mussels to the pan, cover, and cook until they are all open, 4 to 5 minutes. Discard any that do not open.

3. Sprinkle the parsley, tarragon, and tomatoes over the mussels and stir to combine. Right before removing the mussels, sprinkle with the lemon zest.

4. Divide the mussels and liquid among 4 deep pasta bowls and garnish with a dusting of black pepper. Serve with a green salad on the side and pieces of crusty bread for dipping.

NUTRITIONAL INFORMATION Per Serving: 249 cal., 6 g fat, 1 g sat. fat, 14 g carb., 15 g protein, 342 mg sodium, 4 g sugar, 2 g fiber.

SERVES 4

1 tablespoon extra-virgin olive oil

2 shallots, chopped

2 cloves garlic, minced

2 cups dry white wine

1 pound fresh mussels, scrubbed and beards removed

¼ cup chopped fresh flat-leaf parsley

¼ cup chopped fresh tarragon

2 vine-ripened tomatoes, seeded and diced

Zest of 1 lemon

Freshly ground black pepper, to taste

GRILLED GARLIC-LEMON SEA BASS

Lemon and butter do their timeless dance on a richly flavored deep-water fish in this elegant dinner. You won't have to work half the day in the kitchen to create this recipe, but the result will taste like something that just came out of a restaurant. Not to mention, sea bass is ripe with Omega-3 oils and the type of nutrients and vitamins that make a heart doctor happy.

SERVES 4

¼ teaspoon paprika

¼ teaspoon garlic powder

¼ teaspoon onion powder

¼ teaspoon lemon pepper

3 tablespoons unsalted butter

2 cloves garlic, minced

1 teaspoon lemon zest

2 tablespoons finely chopped fresh flat-leaf parsley

2 tablespoons finely chopped fresh thyme

Canola oil, as needed

4 skinless sea bass fillets (4–6 ounces each)

2 lemons, halved

1. In a small bowl, whisk together the paprika, garlic powder, onion powder, and lemon pepper. Set aside.

2. In a small saucepan over medium heat, melt the butter. Add the garlic, lemon zest, parsley, and thyme. Cook until fragrant, about 2 minutes. Pour into a pie plate.

3. Preheat the grill over medium-high heat. Using long-handled tongs and a paper towel moistened with canola oil, lightly coat the grill.

4. Dip the sea bass in the melted butter, evenly coating both sides of each fillet. Sprinkle both sides with the seasoning mixture.

5. Grill, covered for approximately 6 to 8 minutes, or until the fish flakes easily with fork. (Or broil the fillets.) Turn halfway through grilling, basting frequently with the lemon butter sauce. Serve garnished with the lemon halves.

NUTRITIONAL INFORMATION Per Serving: 255 cal., 14 g fat, 5 g sat. fat, 7 g carb., 31 g protein, 170 mg sodium, 0 g sugar, 3 g fiber.

Grilled Garlic-Lemon
Sea Bass

Spicy Ricotta-and-
Zucchini-Stuffed
Baked Shells

SPICY RICOTTA-AND-ZUCCHINI-STUFFED BAKED SHELLS

If you have a craving for pure cheesy, gooey goodness, this is the recipe for you. It's simple and quick to make and a real crowd pleaser. More importantly, it keeps a lid on fats and sugars by using reduced-sugar sauce and low-fat cheeses. Low-fat cheeses are ideal for a baked dish like this, where meltability matters and the texture looms large, but the fat itself won't be missed. Dig in!

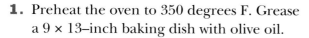

1. Preheat the oven to 350 degrees F. Grease a 9 × 13–inch baking dish with olive oil.

2. Heat the olive oil in a medium nonstick skillet over medium heat. Add the onion, garlic, and carrot, and cook until softened, about 5 minutes.

3. Add the zucchini and cook until soft but not mushy, about 3 minutes. Season the vegetables with salt and pepper. Transfer to a mixing bowl and let cool to room temperature. While it cools, cook the pasta shells according to the package instructions.

4. Add the ricotta, parmesan, and half of the

SERVES 4 TO 6

1 tablespoon extra-virgin olive oil, plus more as needed

1 small yellow onion, chopped

2 cloves garlic, chopped

1 carrot, peeled and finely diced

1 zucchini, finely diced

Salt and freshly ground black pepper, to taste

6 ounces jumbo pasta shells

½ cup low-fat ricotta cheese

¼ cup grated parmesan, plus more as needed

½ cup low-fat grated mozzarella cheese

3 cups jarred low-sugar reduced-sodium spicy marinara sauce

Continued

mozzarella to the cooled vegetables and stir well to combine. Spoon the mixture into the cooked cooled shells. Pour about 1 cup of the sauce into the bottom of the baking dish and arrange the stuffed shells open-side up in the dish. Pour the remaining sauce around the shells and sprinkle the remaining mozzarella and some grated parmesan over the top.

5. Bake until the cheese is melted, bubbling, and beginning to brown, about 40 minutes. Let stand 10 minutes before serving.

NUTRITIONAL INFORMATION Per Serving: 360 cal., 13 g fat, 5 g sat. fat, 42 g carb., 24 g protein, 478 mg sodium, 4 g sugar, 3 g fiber.

HERBED GOAT CHEESE-STUFFED CHICKEN BREASTS

At first glance, it would be easy to underestimate this meal as something rather plain. But that would be a mistake. File this recipe under Special because the melting cheese and bone in the breasts combine to keep the chicken incredibly moist and tender, and the flavors captured in the stuffing permeate all the white meat, making each bite a delight. Chives and lemon add a bright Mediterranean aspect to the dish, and put it over the top.

1. Preheat the oven to 400 degrees F. Grease a 9 × 13–inch baking dish with cooking spray.

2. In a small bowl, combine the cheese, thyme, chives, and freshly ground pepper. Zest the lemon and add it to the cheese. Mix until well combined. Slice the lemon and arrange the slices in a single layer in the baking dish.

3. Use your fingers or a small rubber spatula to loosen the skin on one side of the chicken breasts (leave one side attached to the meat).

4. Divide the goat cheese mixture among the chicken breasts, stuffing it under the skin. Smooth the cheese into an even layer. Brush the breasts all over with olive oil and season them well with salt and pepper.

SERVES 4

Cooking spray

4 ounces goat cheese

1 sprig fresh thyme, leaves only

1 tablespoon chopped fresh chives

Salt and freshly ground black pepper, to taste

1 lemon

4 bone-in, skin on chicken breast halves

1 tablespoon extra-virgin olive oil

Continued

5. Lay the breasts, skin-side up, in the baking dish. Pour about 1 cup of water into the dish. Bake until the chicken is cooked through and the skin is brown, 35 to 40 minutes. (If the skin has not crisped, turn on the broiler and broil until golden brown.)

6. Serve the chicken warm, drizzled with juices from the baking dish.

NUTRITIONAL INFORMATION Per Serving: 347 cal., 21 g fat, 9 g sat. fat, 1 g carb., 36 g protein, 372 mg sodium, 1 g sugar, 0 g fiber.

MEXICAN CHICKEN BURGERS

Mexican burgers? You bet. The wonderful thing about burgers is that they can be reimagined in all kinds of yummy ways, but this is one of the most ingenious and delicious. With just a smattering of spices, a little salsa, and a bun substitute, the humble burger becomes a fiesta of flavor. Use chicken in place of beef for a much leaner, healthier burger. Kids will especially love capturing their "burger" in a tortilla cloak.

1. In a mixing bowl, combine the chicken, pepper, oregano, chili powder, and cumin and mix together gently. (Do not overmix or the burgers will be tough.) Use your hands to divide the mixture into 4 equal portions, and form each portion into an oblong shape, about ½-inch thick.

2. Heat the olive oil in a large nonstick skillet over medium heat. Add the chicken patties, cover the pan, and cook until the burgers are golden brown on the bottom, about 10 minutes.

3. Flip the burgers, cover the pan, and continue cooking until the burgers are golden brown and completely cooked through, 6 to 8 minutes more. Top each burger with 2 tablespoons of the cheese. Remove the pan from the heat, and cover until the cheese is melted.

SERVES 4

1 pound ground chicken

½ teaspoon freshly ground pepper

½ teaspoon dried oregano

½ teaspoon chili powder

¼ teaspoon cumin

1 tablespoon olive oil

½ cup grated pepper jack cheese

⅓ cup plain nonfat Greek yogurt

Zest and juice of 1 lime

Pinch of salt

4 reduced-sodium soft taco flour tortillas

2 cups shredded romaine lettuce, for serving

½ tomato, diced

Continued

4. In a small bowl, combine the yogurt, lime zest and juice, and a pinch of salt.

5. Spread about 1½ tablespoons of the lime yogurt on each tortilla. Position a burger on one side of each tortilla and top each with some shredded lettuce and 2 tablespoons of diced tomatoes. Close the tortillas and serve like a taco.

NUTRITIONAL INFORMATION Per Serving: 407 cal., 14 g fat, 5 g sat. fat, 29 g carb., 39 g protein, 454 mg sodium, 2 g sugar, 2 g fiber.

SQUASH, TOMATO, AND FETA TART

Once you pull this beautiful dish out of the oven, you'll be amazed at just how quick and easy it was to make. Combining some of the best summer vegetables, each bite dances on the tongue. The magic comes together on a light crust that crumbles between the teeth. Its buttery rich, so it's a perfect complement to the garden-fresh veggies and tangy cheese that make up the topping.

1. Preheat the oven to 400 degrees F.

2. On a lightly floured work surface, use a rolling pin to flatten the puff pastry. Transfer the pastry to a baking sheet, and use a sharp knife to score a ½-inch border around the outer edges of the pastry without cutting completely through the pastry.

3. Spread the zucchini, squash, and tomato slices across the pastry, overlapping slightly and placed within the scored border. Brush the vegetables with the olive oil and sprinkle the Italian seasoning over the tart. Scatter the crumbled cheese evenly over the top.

4. Bake the tart until the edges puff and turn golden brown, 20 to 25 minutes. Let stand at least 5 minutes before slicing into 4 large rectangles. Serve with a green salad.

NUTRITIONAL INFORMATION Per Serving: 363 cal., 23 g fat, 11 g sat. fat, 32 g carb., 10 g protein, 474 mg sodium, 5 g sugar, 4 g fiber.

SERVES 4

One sheet frozen puff pastry, thawed

2 thin zucchini, sliced into ⅛-inch thick slices

2 small yellow squash, sliced into ⅛-inch thick slices

8 Roma tomatoes, sliced ⅛-inch thick

1 tablespoon extra-virgin olive oil

½ teaspoon Italian seasoning

2 ounces crumbled feta cheese

ZUCCHINI BOATS WITH MINTED COUSCOUS

Whip up a little Mediterranean magic in this unusual—and unusually delicious—dish. Roasted zucchini serves as the base for a vivid mixture of sweet and savory ingredients topped with a kiss of mint. Roasting the zucchini deepens the natural flavor and gives it an almost melt-in-your-mouth texture. That texture is the perfect partner to the delicate, firm nature of the couscous. This is simple enough for a family meal, but elegant enough for company.

SERVES 4

2 large zucchini (about 8 ounces each), halved lengthwise

½ teaspoon Italian seasoning

Salt and freshly ground black pepper, to taste

Cooking spray

1 cup couscous

1 small red onion, finely chopped

¼ cup golden raisins

¼ cup toasted pine nuts

1¼ cups vegetable broth

¼ cup chopped fresh mint

1. Preheat the oven to 375 degrees F.

2. Use a spoon to scoop out the seeds from each zucchini half. Be careful to keep from cutting all of the way through the flesh. Evenly sprinkle the Italian seasoning over the zucchini halves and season them with salt and pepper. Roast the zucchini on a baking sheet prepared with cooking spray until soft but still holding their shapes, 20 to 25 minutes.

3. While the zucchini roasts, place the couscous in a medium bowl and scatter the onion, raisins, and pine nuts over the surface.

4. In a small saucepan, bring the vegetable broth to a boil and pour it over the couscous. Cover the bowl tightly and let stand for 10 minutes. Uncover and fluff with a fork. Season with salt and pepper, if desired.

Continued

Zucchini Boats with
Minted Couscous

5. Put a zucchini boat on each of the plates. Stir the chopped mint into the warm couscous and fill each zucchini half with one quarter of the couscous. Serve warm.

NUTRITIONAL INFORMATION Per Serving: 161 cal., 5 g fat, 1 g sat. fat, 26 g carb., 6 g protein, 428 mg sodium, 4 g sugar, 4 g fiber.

ITALIAN DINNER FRITTATA

The frittata is the showier, more robust big brother to the omelet. And though an omelet can make a very nice dinner, it can't compare to the one-skillet wonder of a real frittata. This one includes savory turkey sausages crammed with true Italian spices and traditional Italian doses of olive oil, parmesan, and marinara sauce. Eggs are an inviting alternative to pasta, here with an airiness that makes this dish just as good for breakfast or lunch.

1. Preheat the oven to 350 degrees F.

2. Heat the olive oil in an ovenproof, 10-inch nonstick skillet over medium heat. Add the sausage and brown, stirring occasionally. Transfer the sausage to a plate and add the onion to the pan. Cook until softened, about 4 minutes. Return the sausage to the pan along with the red peppers and spread them evenly out in the pan.

3. In a small bowl, whisk the eggs and parmesan. Season with black pepper. Slowly pour the eggs into the pan, distributing them evenly over the sausage and onion and filling all of the crevices.

4. Cook the mixture without disturbing it, until the eggs are set on the bottom and around the sides of the pan. Transfer the pan to the oven and cook until the eggs are completely set, 8 to 10 minutes.

SERVES 4

1 teaspoon extra-virgin olive oil

2 Italian turkey sausages (about 4 ounces total), sliced

1 small yellow onion, sliced

1 large roasted red pepper, thinly sliced

6 large eggs, beaten with 2 tablespoons water

1/8 cup grated parmesan

Freshly ground black pepper, to taste

1 cup low-sodium marinara sauce, warmed

Continued

5. Remove the pan from the oven and let stand for about 1 minute. Using a large rubber spatula, release any edges that are stuck to the pan and slide the frittata onto a plate. Slice into wedges and serve with warm marinara sauce and extra parmesan.

NUTRITIONAL INFORMATION Per Serving: 288 cal., 21 g fat, 7 g sat. fat, 9 g carb., 25 g protein, 478 mg sodium, 5 g sugar, 1 g fiber.

Flank Steak with Red
Pepper Pesto

FLANK STEAK WITH RED PEPPER PESTO

If you don't know about the flank steak, it's time you experienced this wonderful cut of meat. Although this is one of the least expensive steaks in the meat case, it has a deep, true-beef flavor that can't be beat. It's easy to cook and tender when cut against the grain. You might not think that pesto and steak is an ideal combination, but the roasted red-pepper richness puts steak sauce to shame.

SERVES 4 TO 6

For the pesto:

¼ cup whole almonds, toasted

2 cloves garlic, smashed

2 tablespoons extra-virgin olive oil

½ cup roasted red peppers, drained

¼ cup grated parmesan

Pepper, to taste

For the steak:

1 flank steak (about 1½ pounds)

Salt and freshly ground black pepper, to taste

¼ teaspoon garlic powder

1 tablespoon olive oil

1. Preheat a gas grill on high, or heat a grill pan over high heat.

2. Combine the almonds and garlic in the bowl of a food processor. Pulse until finely chopped. With the motor running, add the extra-virgin olive oil and purée until the mixture forms a thick paste.

3. Add the peppers and parmesan, and purée until smooth. Season with pepper to taste. Transfer to a bowl and set aside.

4. Season the steak generously with salt, pepper, and garlic powder. Oil the grill grates or pan with an olive oil–soaked paper towel.

5. Grill the steak, 4 to 5 minutes per side for medium-rare. Transfer the steak to a cutting board, cover, and let stand for 5 to 10 minutes. Thinly slice the steak, cutting across the grain. Drizzle the pesto over the top of the sliced steak and serve.

NUTRITIONAL INFORMATION Per Serving: 359 cal., 24 g fat, 7 g sat. fat, 4 g carb., 33 g protein, 450 mg sodium, 1 g sugar, 1 g fiber.

GREEN CHILE CHICKEN ENCHILADAS

True Mexican cooking sings with flavors boasting the boldness of a Mariachi band, strong, assertive and memorable. That describes these enchiladas to a T, which are authentic enough that they could be served on a restaurant table in Guadalajara. The genuine character comes courtesy of rich, sweet flavors in roasted tomatillos, jalapeño, and onions as well as the deep, tender loveliness of rotisserie chicken meat. Top all that with some pepper jack cheese and you're speaking Spanish in the best accent possible.

1. Preheat the broiler and position an oven rack 6 to 8 inches from the heat source.

2. Spread the whole tomatillos, jalapeño, onion, and garlic on a baking sheet. Drizzle with olive oil and toss to coat. Season with pepper and place under the broiler. Broil until the vegetables are blackened and the tomatillos are very soft and gray green, about 15 minutes.

3. Reduce the heat to 350 degrees F.

4. Transfer the vegetables to the bowl of a food processor. Pulse until fairly smooth. Let stand until cool.

5. Grease an 8 × 10–inch baking dish with cooking spray. Pour some of the tomatillo sauce into the dish, spreading it to coat the bottom.

SERVES 4

1 pound tomatillos, husked and rinsed

1 medium jalapeño

1 small white onion, cut into wedges

3 cloves garlic

1 tablespoon olive oil

Freshly ground black pepper, to taste

Cooking spray

1 rotisserie chicken, meat removed and shredded, skin discarded

4 ounces low-fat pepper jack cheese, grated

Twelve 6-inch corn tortillas

4 tablespoons low-fat plain yogurt, for serving

Continued

6. In a large mixing bowl, combine the chicken and about ⅓ cup of the tomatillo sauce. Toss well to combine. Add half of the grated cheese and stir to combine.

7. Divide the mixture among the tortillas, rolling each into a cigar shape. Place the enchiladas, seam-side down, in the baking dish. They should be touching.

8. Pour the remaining tomatilla sauce around the sides of the enchiladas and over the top. Scatter the remaining cheese over the surface. Bake until the sauce is very hot and bubbly and the cheese is melted, 15 to 20 minutes. Let stand 5 minutes before serving with a dollop of yogurt on top.

NUTRITIONAL INFORMATION Per Serving: 406 cal., 22 g fat, 6 g sat. fat, 45 g carb., 36 g protein, 438 mg sodium, 3 g sugar, 5 g fiber.

Green Chile
Chicken Enchiladas

BEEF TENDERLOIN WITH CREAMY SPINACH

This is a country club favorite that can make any dinner a special occasion. Tenderloin, as its name would suggest, is just about the most tender cut of meat that you can find. Center-cut tenderloins are preferred, but any steak produced from this section is going to be delicious—even more so when paired with simple-and-satisfying creamed spinach. Cooked to perfection, the greens have a melt-in-your-mouth consistency that will leave you wanting more.

SERVES 4

1 tablespoon extra-virgin olive oil

4 beef tenderloin steaks (6–7 ounces each, about 1½ inches thick)

Salt and freshly ground black pepper, to taste

1 tablespoon unsalted butter

1 tablespoon all-purpose flour

½ cup soy creamer

½ teaspoon mustard powder

Pinch freshly grated nutmeg

1 large shallot, sliced

1 pound spinach leaves

1. Heat the olive oil in a medium nonstick skillet over medium-high heat. Season the steaks on both sides with salt and pepper and place them in the pan. Cook until seared and golden, turning once (about 4 minutes per side for medium). Transfer the steaks to a plate and cover with a tent made of aluminum foil to keep warm.

2. Melt the butter in a small saucepan over medium heat. Add the flour and cook for 1 minute. Whisk in the soy creamer, mustard powder, nutmeg, salt, and pepper. Cook until the sauce begins to bubble and thicken, 2 to 3 minutes. Remove from the heat.

3. Add the shallots to the skillet used to cook the steaks. Cook until softened, about 3 minutes.

Continued

Beef Tenderloin with
Creamy Spinach

4. Add the spinach, cover the pan, and cook for 1 to 2 minutes until the spinach wilts. Transfer the spinach to a colander and shake it a few times to remove the excess moisture.

5. Return the spinach to the skillet over medium heat. Pour the sauce over the spinach and stir. Season with additional salt and pepper to taste. Cook until hot and bubbly, about 1 minute. Serve the steaks with the creamy spinach on the side while still hot.

NUTRITIONAL INFORMATION Per Serving: 472 cal., 23 g fat, 7 g sat. fat, 9 g carb., 65 g protein, 385 mg sodium, 0 g sugar, 2 g fiber.

SIRLOIN STEAK WITH PEPPERS AND ONIONS

Every once in a while we all need a good hearty dinner that speaks to the soul as much as the stomach. This is it. The rich, filling taste of a high-quality steak cut such as sirloin not only balances strong flavor and appealing tenderness, it delivers ample amounts of iron, protein, and other key nutrients. The peppers and onions round out the dish, adding garden goodness full of Italian-style spices. The aroma alone is better than a dinner bell.

1. In a small bowl, stir together the salt, pepper, paprika, and garlic powder. Pat the steak dry with paper towels and sprinkle the spice mixture evenly over both sides of the meat, patting it in with your hands. Let stand for 30 minutes at room temperature.

2. Heat the olive oil in a large skillet over medium-high heat. Add the steak to the pan and cook without moving it. Cook until the underside is golden, 3 to 4 minutes.

3. Flip the steak and cook for an additional 3 minutes for medium, or until a thermometer inserted into the thickest part reads 135–140 degrees F. Transfer the steak to a cutting board and cover tightly with aluminum foil to keep warm.

SERVES 4

½ teaspoon salt

½ teaspoon freshly ground black pepper, plus more as needed

½ teaspoon paprika

¼ teaspoon garlic powder

1½ pound boneless sirloin steak

2 tablespoons olive oil

1 yellow onion, sliced lengthwise

3 cloves garlic, sliced

1 tablespoon tomato paste

½ teaspoon Italian seasoning

½ cup dry red wine

1 red bell pepper, stemmed, seeded, and thinly sliced

Continued

Sirloin Steak with
Peppers and Onions

4. Add the onion and garlic to the skillet and stir until softened, about 4 minutes. Add the tomato paste and Italian seasoning and stir until the paste coats the vegetables and begins to caramelize, about 2 minutes.

5. Add the red wine and stir, scraping up any browned bits in the pan. Add the bell peppers and cover. Cook until the bell peppers are soft, about 5 minutes. Remove the lid and continue cooking until any liquid in the pan has mostly evaporated.

6. Add the vinegar. Stir and taste and add salt and pepper as needed. Remove the pan from the heat.

7. Slice the steak across the grain on a diagonal and divide the slices among 4 plates. Use tongs to spread the peppers and onion over the steak and serve warm.

NUTRITIONAL INFORMATION Per Serving: 515 cal., 27 g fat, 9 g sat. fat, 11 g carb., 47 g protein, 405 mg sodium, 3 g sugar, 2 g fiber.

1 yellow bell pepper, stemmed, seeded, and thinly sliced

1 tablespoon balsamic vinegar

VEGETABLE TOSTADAS

The beauty of the tostada is that it comes with its own crunchy built-in plate. The toppings traditionally rely on spices, cheese, and beans to give the meat a lot of character, but this version blends those stunningly tasty elements with vegetarian bliss. Combine classic tostada ingredients with sturdy squash and sweet red onions and you have a salad alternative that leaves any salad in the dust.

SERVES 4

1 medium yellow squash, cut into ¼-inch thick slices

1 medium zucchini, cut into ¼-inch thick slices

1 red onion, sliced into half moons about ¼-inch thick

2 tablespoons olive oil

1 clove garlic, minced

½ teaspoon chili powder

½ teaspoon dried oregano

¼ teaspoon cumin

Black pepper, to taste

One 14-ounce can reduced-sodium refried beans, warmed

8 crispy corn tostada shells

1 ounce queso fresco, crumbled

1 avocado, thinly sliced

½ tomato, diced

4 scallions, sliced

1. Preheat the oven to 400 degrees F.

2. Spread the yellow squash, zucchini, and onion slices on a baking sheet. In a small bowl, whisk together the olive oil, garlic, chili powder, oregano, cumin, and pepper until emulsified. Drizzle the mixture evenly over the vegetables and toss to coat.

3. Roast the vegetables until soft and beginning to brown, about 20 minutes. Turn several times with a spatula during cooking.

4. Spread about 3 tablespoons of the beans on each tostada shell. Divide the vegetables evenly among the tostada shells and scatter the cheese over the top of each. Lay 2 slices of avocado on each tostada and top with about 1 tablespoon of diced tomatoes. Garnish with scallions and serve.

NUTRITIONAL INFORMATION Per Serving: 409 cal., 25 g fat, 6 g sat. fat, 42 g carb., 15 g protein, 433 mg sodium, 4 g sugar, 10 g fiber.

Vegetable Tostadas

BONE-HUGGING CHILI

The truth about chili is that, because of all the spices and flavors, you really don't need any extra fat. That's why this recipe focuses on lean ground beef—the leaner the better. The meat in the dish actually becomes a flavor sponge, and you never have to worry about it drying out because it's cooking in so much moisture.

SERVES 8

1.5 pounds lean ground beef (or substitute ground turkey)

1 teaspoon olive oil

½ medium yellow onion, finely diced

½ stalk celery, finely diced

½ green bell pepper, finely diced

1 clove garlic, finely minced

⅓ cup salt-free chili seasoning mix

Two 14.5-ounce cans reduced-sodium diced tomatoes

One and a half 8-ounce cans reduced-sodium tomato sauce

One 16-ounce can reduced-sodium black beans, drained

One 15.5-ounce can reduced-sodium kidney beans, drained

1. Brown the beef in a Dutch oven over medium-high heat. Drain well and set aside the beef. Pour off any grease remaining in the Dutch oven.

2. Heat the olive oil in the Dutch oven over medium-high heat. Swirl to coat the bottom.

3. Add the onion, celery, and pepper. Sauté until the onion is translucent and the celery and pepper are softened. Add the garlic and cook until fragrant, about 1 to 2 minutes.

4. Return the beef to the Dutch oven. Sprinkle with the seasoning mix and stir until the beef and vegetables are coated. Sauté for 1 or 2 additional minutes.

5. Stir in the diced tomatoes and tomato sauce. Add the beans and their liquid. Bring to a boil, stirring occasionally. Cover, reduce the heat to a simmer, and cook for 15 minutes, stirring occasionally. Serve hot.

NUTRITIONAL INFORMATION Per Serving: 346 cal., 9 g fat, 3 g sat. fat, 29 g carb., 45 g protein, 468 mg sodium, 10 g sugar, 10 g fiber.

TRISTÉ'S QUICK SLOPPY JOES

While my wife makes this specialty, my entire family is buzzing about desperately trying to dip in a spoon for a sneak taste. It has all the things we love about food and best of all, it's so quick and easy to make. How about some fun on a bun? There should be room in every kitchen for a purely delicious, enjoyable, over-the-top family meal. So here it is. A cascade of wonderful flavors gives this crowd-pleaser its well-rounded character, and it's got all the makings you'd expect in a classic sloppy Joe. But throwing a little maple syrup into the mix puts a curve on the traditional standard. There's a marked balance of sweet and spicy that really puts this dish over the top, and makes it a cold-weather happy meal like no other.

1. In a medium bowl, combine the tomatoes, ketchup, Worcestershire sauce, mustard, vinegar, maple syrup, chili powder, and cumin. Whisk the sauce to combine and set aside.

2. In a large skillet over medium-high heat, brown the ground turkey. Drain well and transfer the turkey to a bowl. Set aside.

3. Heat the olive oil in a large skillet over medium heat. Add the carrot and sauté until soft. Add the bell peppers and onion and cook until soft and translucent. Add the garlic and sauté until fragrant, about 1 to 2 minutes.

SERVES 6 TO 8

One 14.5-ounce can reduced-sodium diced tomatoes

1 cup organic ketchup (for lower sodium option, use no-salt ketchup)

½ tablespoon Worcestershire sauce

½ tablespoon Dijon or brown mustard

1 teaspoon red wine vinegar

2 tablespoons pure maple syrup

1 tablespoon chili powder

Continued

1 teaspoon cumin

1¼ pounds lean ground turkey

2 teaspoons olive oil

1 large carrot, finely diced

1 cup finely diced red, yellow,
   or orange bell pepper

1 medium yellow onion,
   finely diced

2 cloves garlic, minced

8 whole-wheat hamburger
   buns, toasted

4. Reduce the temperature to low and add the sauce. Simmer for 10 minutes, stirring frequently. Add the ground turkey, stir to combine, and simmer for 5 minutes or until warmed through.

5. Spoon the mixture onto the toasted hamburger buns.

NUTRITIONAL INFORMATION Per Serving: 351 cal., 22 g fat, 5 g sat. fat, 41 g carb., 23 g protein, 545 mg sodium, 20 g sugar, 93 g fiber.

EGGPLANT AND ASPARAGUS ROLLATINI

Bread and bake slices of eggplant and wrap them around a luscious filling for a dish that will appeal even to those who are a little iffy about the purple vegetable. The secret is the cheese—you don't have to use a lot when the flavors are distinctive, as in the provolone and parmesan used here. Baking is a much healthier alternative than the more traditional pan-frying, but the eggplant still ends up with an inviting flavor coating.

1. Preheat the oven to 375 degrees F. Grease a baking sheet and a 9 inch × 13–inch baking dish with olive oil.

2. In a small bowl, combine the olive oil, garlic powder, and a pinch pepper. Stir until thoroughly mixed.

3. Use a pastry brush to brush both sides of the eggplant slices with the seasoned olive oil. Lay them on the baking sheet and bake for 15 minutes, until soft but still holding their shape. Remove from the oven and let stand until cool enough to handle.

4. Divide the asparagus into 8 equal-sized bundles. Lay the eggplant slices on a work surface and position the asparagus bundles on them crosswise. Lay a few sticks of cheese on each bundle and roll the eggplant up to enclose the asparagus.

SERVES 4

2 tablespoons extra-virgin olive oil, plus more as needed

¼ teaspoon garlic powder

Freshly ground black pepper, to taste

1 large globe eggplant, sliced lengthwise into 8 slices, each about ¼-inch thick

12 ounces asparagus spears, trimmed

3 ounces aged provolone, cut into matchsticks

1½ cups jarred reduced-sodium marinara sauce

¼ cup grated parmesan, plus more for serving

Continued

5. Line up the rollatini in the baking dish. Cover evenly with sauce and sprinkle with parmesan.

6. Bake until the sauce is bubbling and hot, the cheese is melting, and the asparagus are cooked through, about 15 minutes. Serve warm with extra parmesan on the side.

NUTRITIONAL INFORMATION Per Serving: 273 cal., 20 g fat, 7 g sat. fat, 24 g carb., 12 g protein, 465 mg sodium, 11 g sugar, 5 g fiber.

DR. IAN'S SWEET BARBECUE STEAKS

This is the dish where I've earned my stripes with my family. Sometimes the only thing that will truly hit the spot is a hearty cut of meat. A rib-eye steak is one of the heartiest—and most flavorful—cuts you're likely to find, and it's rich in iron and protein to boot. You may have to find a butcher to get a Prime grade cut, but it's well worth the extra effort and expense because the flavor of Prime beef is unparalleled. Of course, any cut of meat can be helped along by the right unique barbecue sauce that blends the savory with the sweet and gives the tongue a lot to think about. I really love barbecue and this is something I prepare for my family that they absolutely look forward to every time I make it. Some would call this a "cheat" meal, but I call it great fun. Don't feel guilty at all. Enjoy every bite!

1. Preheat the broiler.

2. Poke holes in both sides of each steak, using a fork. Season the steaks on both sides with the meat tenderizer. Coat each side of the steak with an equal amount of Worcestershire sauce. Set aside for 5 minutes.

3. Broil the steaks in a pan with a rack. Cook for about 4 minutes on each side. Remove the steaks and reduce the heat to 350 degrees F.

SERVES 2

Two 5-ounce rib-eye steaks (USDA Prime, dry aged, well-marbled)

¼ teaspoon seasoned meat tenderizer

1 teaspoon Worcestershire sauce

¼ cup Sweet Baby Ray's Honey Barbecue Sauce

½ teaspoon honey

½ teaspoon brown sugar

Continued

4. In a small bowl, combine the barbecue sauce with the honey and brown sugar. Blot one side of each steak dry using a paper towel. Baste each steak thoroughly with the barbecue sauce mixture.

5. Bake the steaks in the oven for 2 minutes, and then baste with remaining barbecue sauce mixture. Bake the steaks until the sauce is glazed on the meat and no longer runny.

NUTRITIONAL INFORMATION Per Serving: 483 cal., 31 g fat, 12 g sat. fat, 23 g carb., 33 g protein, 554 mg sodium, 20 g sugar, 0 g fiber.

CREOLE TROUT FILLETS WITH COLLARD GREENS

In the true Creole tradition, this dish includes collard greens cooked to the point of perfection with nothing more than a scattering of seasoning, some pepper, and a spritz of lemon. The buttery nature of this green hides the fact that is a superfood jam-packed with vitamins and nutrients.

1. Fill a large pot with 1 inch of water and position a vegetable steamer basket inside of it. Bring the water to a simmer over medium-high heat.

2. Add the collard greens and onion. Cover and cook for 10 minutes, or until the greens are very soft. Remove the greens and season with pepper to taste. Sprinkle the lemon zest over top. Set aside and keep warm.

3. Season the flesh side of the trout fillets with salt and pepper. Sprinkle the Creole seasoning evenly over both sides of the fish.

4. Heat the olive oil in a large nonstick skillet over medium-high heat. Add the fish, flesh-side down. Cook until the fish just begins to brown, 1 to 2 minutes. Using a thin spatula, flip the fillets and cook until the skin begins to crisp, about 2 minutes.

5. Divide the greens among 4 serving plates and place a fillet on top of each. Serve with lemon wedges.

NUTRITIONAL INFORMATION Per Serving 383 cal., 19 g fat, 5 g sat. fat, 7 g carb., 44 g protein, 388 mg sodium, 1 g sugar, 3 g fiber.

SERVES 4

For the collard greens:

1 large bunch collard greens, stems removed and leaves thinly sliced

1 small red onion, sliced

Freshly ground black pepper, to taste

Zest of ½ lemon

For the trout:

Four 6-ounce skin-on trout fillets

Salt and freshly ground black pepper, to taste

½ teaspoon Creole seasoning

2 tablespoons extra-virgin olive oil

1 lemon, cut into 4 wedges, for serving

Ma's Easy
Eggplant Parmesan

MA'S EASY EGGPLANT PARMESAN

This recipe has been handed down from my grandmother, who knew her way around the kitchen like it was nobody's business. When she made this dish, calls quickly made their way around the family, and everyone understood that it was best to get to her house before it was gone. When it comes to comfort foods, few can rival the seductive wonders of Old World parmigiana. The eggplant here stands in for the more common chicken, but it's actually a better choice in this particular dish. The cooking gives the eggplant a lovely soft texture and all the flavors in the dish seem to concentrate in the layer of eggplant. Couple that with the luxurious melted cheese and a tomato sauce that is pure delight on the tongue and you'll discover why this is such a favorite in Italian kitchens across the country. It also stands up to freezing, making it a wonderful make-ahead dish for special occasions. My mother continues to carry the banner of this family recipe that just keeps us shaking our heads after every rich, mouthwatering bite.

1. Preheat the oven to 350 degrees F.

2. Lightly coat the bottom of a 9 x 13–inch baking pan with olive oil, then lay the eggplant in the baking pan in a single layer and brush with olive oil. Bake until the eggplant is soft, about 20 minutes.

3. While the eggplant bakes, heat the olive oil in a large saucepan over medium-high heat. Add the onion and cook until it begins to soften.

SERVES 8

2 tablespoons olive oil

3 large eggplants, peeled and cut into slices ½- to ¼-inch thick

1 small yellow onion, chopped

2–3 cloves garlic, smashed and chopped

½ teaspoon dried oregano

Continued

½ teaspoon Italian seasoning

½ teaspoon kosher salt

½ teaspoon freshly ground black pepper

One 28-ounce can low-sodium tomato sauce

One 6-ounce can low-sodium tomato paste

4–6 leaves of fresh basil, julienned

2–4 sprigs thyme, leaves only

One 16-ounce package fresh mozzarella cheese, sliced very thin

One 15-ounce container fat-free ricotta cheese

¾ cup grated low-sodium parmesan cheese

4. Add the garlic and cook for one minute, but do not let the garlic burn. Add the oregano, Italian seasoning, salt, and black pepper.

5. Stir in the tomato sauce and tomato paste. Add the basil and thyme and stir to blend. Season with salt and pepper to taste. Reduce heat to a simmer, and simmer until thickened.

6. Spread a thin layer of sauce on the bottom of another 9 × 13–inch x 1 inch baking pan. Place layer of eggplant slices on top of sauce and scatter mozzarella slices over the eggplant. Sprinkle four tablespoons of parmesan over eggplant.

7. Cover with another thin layer of sauce. Repeat the process and cover the top layer with sauce. Sprinkle parmesan liberally over the top, and bake until the cheese is melted and the eggplant is heated through, about 35 minutes.

NUTRITIONAL INFORMATION Per Serving: 317 cal., 30 g fat, 15 g sat. fat, 23 g carb., 21 g protein, 260 mg sodium, 12 g sugar, 8 g fiber.

ARTICHOKE AND SWISS CHEESE-STUFFED PORK CHOPS

File this under unusual flavor combinations that work incredibly well together. It's a little bit surprising how well the artichoke and tangy cheese in this dish mesh; you may never want to serve them separately again. The sharp flavors infiltrate the mild pork, seasoning the meat as you cook the pork chops. Word of caution though—keep an eye on the chops during cooking; the pork should be cooked through but not overcooked or the chops will be tough.

1. Preheat the oven to 400 degrees F.

2. Use a sharp, thin knife to slice the pork chops in half horizontally without slicing all of the way through.

3. In the bowl of a food processor, pulse the artichokes until they are finely chopped, then transfer them to a large bowl. Add the cracker crumbs and cheese. Drizzle enough of the artichoke marinade over the stuffing to moisten it.

4. Open the pocket you cut in each pork chop, and fill with the stuffing. Skewer the pockets with toothpicks to close them. Season both sides of the chops with salt and pepper.

5. Heat the olive oil in a large, ovenproof, nonstick skillet over medium-high heat. Add the pork chops and cook until browned, 3 to 4 minutes. Flip the chops and transfer the pan to the oven.

SERVES 4

4 boneless pork loin chops, about 1-inch thick

½ cup marinated artichokes, drained, liquid reserved

12 whole-wheat crackers (about 1-inch square), crushed

1 ounce Swiss cheese, finely diced

Salt and freshly ground black pepper, to taste

½ tablespoon extra-virgin olive oil

1½ cups cooked white rice, for serving

6. Cook until the bottoms of the chops are golden and the chops are completely cooked through, 10 to 12 minutes. Remove from the oven and remove the toothpicks. Serve with cooked rice.

NUTRITIONAL INFORMATION Per Serving: 522 cal., 29 g fat, 9 g sat. fat, 34 g carb., 45 g protein, 444 mg sodium, 3 g sugar, 1 g fiber.

Chicken, Roasted Pepper,
and Spinach Quesadillas

CHICKEN, ROASTED PEPPER, AND SPINACH QUESADILLAS

Quesadillas have always been fairly simple creations, but that doesn't mean you can't dress them up a little. And what better way to do that than to add the smoky goodness of roasted red pepper and a boost of iron, vitamins, and minerals courtesy of spinach. Rotisserie chicken is a great alternative to plain white meat in this cheesy favorite because it adds a rich deep-roasted note that elevates the other flavors.

SERVES 4

8 whole-wheat tortillas (for lower sodium use corn tortilla instead)

2 ounces grated Monterey Jack cheese

1½ cups shredded rotisserie chicken meat (about 1 chicken)

1 large roasted red pepper, thinly sliced

One 10-ounce box frozen chopped spinach, thawed and drained

Cooking spray

2 cups arugula, dressed with fresh lemon juice to taste

1. Preheat the oven to 200 degrees F.

2. Lay 4 tortillas on a work surface. Spread half of the cheese evenly over the tortillas, followed by the chicken and red pepper strips.

3. Wrap the spinach in a towel and squeeze it firmly to remove all the excess moisture. Spread the spinach evenly over the chicken and peppers. Evenly scatter the rest of the cheese over each quesadilla and top with the remaining tortillas.

4. Coat a large nonstick skillet with cooking spray and heat it over medium heat. Cook a quesadilla until the bottom is golden, 3 to 4 minutes. Spray the top of the quesadilla with cooking spray and carefully flip it. Cook until the bottom is light golden brown, 2 to 3 minutes more. Transfer the quesadilla to a baking sheet and keep warm in the oven. Repeat with the remaining 3 quesadillas.

5. Cut the quesadillas into quarters and divide among 4 serving plates. Serve with the lemon-dressed arugula.

NUTRITIONAL INFORMATION Per Serving: 246 cal., 19 g fat, 7 g sat. fat, 35 g carb., 32 g protein, 562 mg sodium, 0 g sugar, 7 g fiber.

Grilled Barbecue Chicken and Red Onion Pizza

GRILLED BARBECUE CHICKEN AND RED ONION PIZZA

Forget about takeout; making your own pizza is cheaper, easier, healthier, and definitely more fun. This family favorite is an exciting upgrade from a plain old cheese-and-pepperoni pie, with out-of-control flavors and under-control sugars. By topping the pizza with grilled chicken, you combine the best of a cookout and a pizza party. Built on a prebaked pizza crust, this amazing dish can be put together and out of the oven in less than 45 minutes!

1. Preheat a grill pan over medium-high heat.

2. Spray the chicken breasts with cooking spray and season them with the salt and pepper. Grill the chicken without moving the breasts until grill marks appear, about 5 minutes. Flip the chicken and cook for 5 minutes more, until completely cooked through and an instant-read thermometer reads 165 degrees F.

3. Transfer the chicken to a plate and brush both sides with barbecue sauce. Let stand until cool enough to handle. Cut the chicken breasts crosswise into thin slices.

4. Preheat the oven to 425 degrees F.

5. Put the pizza crust on a pizza pan or baking sheet. Spread the remaining barbecue sauce over the surface of the crust.

SERVES 4

2 skinless, boneless chicken breasts

Olive oil cooking spray

Salt and freshly ground black pepper, to taste (slight pinch of salt)

½ cup sugar-free barbecue sauce

One 12-inch, prebaked, low-sodium, whole-wheat pizza crust

¼ cup grated Monterey Jack cheese

¼ cup grated mozzarella cheese

1 large red onion, julienned

6 large fresh basil leaves, thinly sliced

Continued

6. Sprinkle ¾ of each cheese evenly over the sauce. Arrange the sliced chicken in a single layer over the crust and scatter the slivered onion evenly over it. Sprinkle the rest of the cheese over the pizza and bake until the cheese is melted and the sauce is bubbly and hot, 10 to 12 minutes.

7. Slide the pizza onto a cutting board and cut into wedges. Sprinkle the sliced basil over the top and serve.

NUTRITIONAL INFORMATION Per Serving: 437 cal., 11 g fat, 6 g sat. fat, 45 g carb., 29 g protein, 451 mg sodium, 4 g sugar, 6 g fiber.

CHICKEN AND MUSHROOMS

A little classical French panache creates a decadent mushroom-and-white-wine sauce that elevates chicken to an art form. As wonderful as this sauce is, it performs its magic with surprisingly small amounts of carbs, fats, or sugars. The secret lies in making the most of the spices in the dish and including modest amounts of high-flavor ingredients. But the health benefits will be a far second to flavors that are sure to draw oohs and ahs from everyone around the table. Even though this is easy enough to whip up on any given weeknight, the dish is special enough for your next dinner party or birthday meal.

1. Preheat the oven to 250 degrees F.

2. Place each chicken breast half between 2 sheets of waxed paper and pound them to about ½-inch thick, using a rolling pin or wooden mallet. Season the pounded breasts with salt and pepper.

3. Heat the canola oil in a large nonstick skillet over medium-high heat. Cook the chicken for 4 minutes on each side, or until cooked through. Transfer the chicken to a baking sheet and keep warm in the oven.

4. Add shallots and mushrooms to the skillet and sauté for 3 minutes, stirring occasionally. Add the wine and bring to a boil. Cook until almost all of the liquid evaporates.

SERVES 4

Four 6-ounce skinless, boneless chicken-breast halves

½ teaspoon salt

¼ teaspoon freshly ground black pepper

2 teaspoons canola oil

¼ cup chopped shallots

1 cup sliced button mushrooms

½ cup dry white wine

1 tablespoon all-purpose flour

½ cup fat-free, lower-sodium chicken broth

½ teaspoon chopped fresh basil

Continued

1 teaspoon minced fresh thyme

¼ teaspoon chopped fresh flat-leaf parsley

1 tablespoon unsalted butter

5. Add the flour and cook for 1 minute, stirring frequently. Add the broth and bring to a boil. Add the basil, thyme, and parsley. Cook until the sauce is reduced and slightly thickened. Remove the skillet from the heat and stir in the butter.

6. Divide the chicken between four plates and cover with the mushroom sauce. Serve warm.

NUTRITIONAL INFORMATION Per Serving: 229 cal., 9 g fat, 3 g sat. fat, 5 g carb., 26 g protein, 285 mg sodium, 0 g sugar, 0 g fiber.

PRETZEL-CRUSTED FISH STICKS WITH EASY COLESLAW

Why turn to highly processed, low-nutrition fish sticks when you can make your own uniquely flavored versions without breaking a sweat? Each of these delicacies is made from a pure cod fillet, brimming with heart-healthy Omega 3 oils. But it's the crunch that will bring everyone to the table. Not only does the pretzel crust create a crackly surface, the cabbage slaw's snap is refreshing, light, and tart.

SERVES 4

1 pound fresh cod fillets, cut into long, thin pieces

Salt and freshly ground black pepper, to taste

¾ cup unsalted mini pretzels, finely crushed

1 large egg, beaten

¼ cup low-fat mayonnaise

1 teaspoon cider vinegar

¼ teaspoon celery seeds

3 cups shredded cabbage

1 lemon, cut into wedges

1. Preheat the oven to 400 degrees F.

2. Pat the fish pieces dry and season with salt and pepper. Spread the pretzel crumbs on a plate. Dredge the fish pieces lightly in the egg and then press in the pretzel crumbs, shaking off any excess. Transfer the breaded fish to a baking sheet.

3. Bake the fish until it is golden brown and cooked through, about 10 minutes.

4. In a small bowl, combine the mayonnaise, vinegar, celery seeds, and about ½ teaspoon of salt.

5. In a mixing bowl, place the cabbage. Pour the dressing over the cabbage and toss to coat. Let stand at least 10 minutes.

5. Serve the warm fish sticks with lemon wedges and the slaw on the side.

NUTRITIONAL INFORMATION Per Serving: 395 cal., 25 g fat, 5 g sat. fat, 23 g carb., 24 g protein, 465 mg sodium, 1 g sugar, 3 g fiber.

Pretzel-Crusted
Fish Sticks with Easy
Coleslaw

ROASTED TURKEY SAUSAGES
WITH SMASHED GERMAN POTATOES

Grab the gusto with a meal that would be right at home in a beer garden. Bratwursts are a hearty traditional German sausage, and substituting turkey for the more common beef or pork makes for a leaner sausage. But because a brat's flavor is largely a result of the many spices used in the sausage, a turkey brat is every bit as delicious and filling as any other.

SERVES 4

12 ounces baby red potatoes, halved

2 tablespoons extra-virgin olive oil

Freshly ground black pepper, to taste

4 reduced-sodium turkey sausages

6 sweet gherkin pickles, diced

2 tablespoons brine from the pickle jar

½ teaspoon whole-grain mustard

Chopped fresh flat-leaf parsley, for garnish

1. Preheat the oven to 375 degrees F.

2. Spread the potatoes on a nonstick baking sheet and drizzle with the olive oil. Toss to coat the potatoes and the pan with the oil. Season the potatoes with the pepper. Pierce the sausages with a fork, add them to the pan, and toss them to coat with the oil.

3. Bake the bratwursts turning them every 5 minutes. Cook until the potatoes are cooked through and the bratwursts are golden brown and cooked through, about 20 minutes.

4. Transfer the potatoes and any liquid on the baking sheet to a mixing bowl. Add the diced pickles. In a small bowl, whisk the pickle brine and mustard, and drizzle over the potatoes. Mash the potatoes with a masher until coarse.

5. Serve the bratwurst warm with the potatoes on the side sprinkled with parsley.

NUTRITIONAL INFORMATION Per Serving: 377 cal., 17 g fat, 4 g sat. fat, 25 g carb., 20 g protein, 345 mg sodium, 17 g sugar, 3 g fiber.

Roasted Turkey
Sausages
with Smashed German
Potatoes

SIDES

Making Your Meal Complete

What you choose to complement your main dish can make all the difference in keeping you shredding. Your side dish can add flavor, nutrients, and satisfaction. Some of these dishes can be eaten as an entire meal if you increase the portions, while others are just enough to fill out the plate. Side dishes are a great opportunity to be adventurous and whimsical, even experimental. I've always believed that while the focus tends to be on the main dish, the sides are what can make or break a meal.

The best side dishes tend to be simple. This also means you have a chance to play with the ingredients a little. Trying a new spice or experimenting with a different herb is fair game. Take license and have fun, but remember there's an expected portion size difference between a side and main, so keep this in mind as you begin cooking. Now it's time to dig in!

AVOCADO, GRAPEFRUIT, AND RED ONION SALAD WITH MINT

It would be hard for any salad to match the blast of freshness this dish brings to the table. But that's just the first of its attractions. Satiny texture? Check? Appealing crunch? Check. Tantalizing tartness with just a hint of fruity sweetness? You bet. The amazing thing is that this salad achieves so much in terms of flavor and texture with so few ingredients—and meager amounts of calories, fat, and sodium.

SERVES 4

2 large ruby red grapefruit

1 small red onion, thinly sliced

Salt and freshly ground pepper, to taste

1 ripe avocado, peeled, pitted, and cubed

½ teaspoon honey

2 teaspoons extra-virgin olive oil

¼ cup fresh mint leaves, torn

1. Stand the grapefruit on one end and, using a very sharp knife, cut the peel and pith cleanly away from the flesh by running the knife down the contour of the fruit. In a bowl, cut the membranes on both sides to free the flesh suprêmes. Squeeze the membranes to remove the juice. Repeat with the second grapefruit.

2. Place the onion in a small bowl, sprinkle salt over the slices, and drizzle with a little of the grapefruit juice from the membranes. Let stand for 10 minutes and then drain. (This will remove the bite from the raw onion.)

3. Arrange the grapefruit and avocado on a serving platter and scatter the onion slices over the top.

4. In a small bowl, combine the honey and remaining grapefruit juice, and whisk until incorporated. Add the olive oil and whisk until incorporated. Season with salt and pepper to taste.

5. Drizzle the dressing over the salad. Scatter the torn mint leaves over top and serve.

NUTRITIONAL INFORMATION Per Serving: 160 cal., 10 g fat, 1 g sat. fat, 18 g carb., 2 g protein, 162 mg sodium, 8 g sugar, 5 g fiber.

Avocado, Grapefruit, and
Red Onion Salad with Mint

CREAMY POLENTA

Polenta is the chameleon of grains; made from cornmeal, it can be served loose as the consistency of oatmeal, or baked, fried, or even grilled into a bread-like sturdiness. This dish taps the elegant side of polenta, creating a super-smooth, rich body that showcases just a handful of simple yet pleasing flavors. A dash of buttermilk adds a faint intriguing tang to a dish that is otherwise savory and risotto-like.

1. In a medium saucepan over medium-high heat, combine the broth, salt, and garlic powder. Bring to a boil. Slowly drizzle the polenta into the liquid while constantly whisking.

2. Cook and continue stirring constantly with a wooden spoon until the mixture thickens noticeably, 2 to 3 minutes. Add the buttermilk and stir until the liquid is completely absorbed.

3. Remove the pan from the heat and stir in the parmesan. Season with pepper to taste. Serve warm.

NUTRITIONAL INFORMATION Per Serving: 107 cal., 3 g fat, 1 g sat. fat, 13 g carb., 5 g protein, 451 mg sodium, 3 g sugar, 0 g fiber.

SERVES 4

3½ cups low-sodium vegetable broth
Pinch of garlic powder
Pinch of salt
1 cup instant polenta
½ cup low-fat buttermilk
¼ cup finely grated low-sodium parmesan
Freshly ground black pepper, to taste

ISRAELI COUSCOUS

WITH RAISINS, PINE NUTS, AND ROASTED SHALLOTS

Israeli couscous—sometimes sold as pearl or pearled couscous—is larger than the more common variety; each grain is about the size of a peppercorn. With an appealingly light nuttiness, Israeli couscous is high in fiber and low on the glycemic index. The understated flavor is ideal with a combination of sweet and savory, like the pine nuts and raisins in this dish. But it's the contrast between crunch and softness that keeps every bite of this dish interesting.

SERVES 4

1 large shallot

1 small clove garlic

2 teaspoons olive oil

Salt and freshly ground black pepper, to taste

2 cups Israeli couscous

2¼ cups low-sodium chicken stock (or substitute low-sodium vegetable broth)

⅓ cup golden raisins

¼ cup pine nuts, toasted

4 scallions, thinly sliced

1. Preheat the oven to 400 degrees F.

2. Place the shallot and garlic on a piece of aluminum foil. Drizzle with 1 teaspoon of the olive oil, season with salt and pepper, and wrap up in the foil.

3. Roast until the shallot is very soft, about 30 minutes. Carefully open the foil and let sit until cool enough to handle, then chop the shallot together with the garlic.

4. Heat the remaining olive oil in a medium saucepan over medium heat. Add the couscous and stir until it begins to turn light golden brown, 5 to 6 minutes.

5. Add the stock and chopped shallot mix. Season with a pinch of salt, and bring to a boil. Reduce the heat to a simmer, cover, and cook until the liquid has been absorbed, about 10 minutes.

6. Soak the raisins in hot water for 10 minutes and then drain. Remove the lid from the couscous and stir in the raisins, pine nuts, and scallions. Season with salt and pepper to taste. Serve warm.

NUTRITIONAL INFORMATION Per Serving: 396 cal., 7 g fat, 1 g sat. fat, 73 g carb., 13 g protein, 195 mg sodium, 9 g sugar, 9 g fiber.

Israeli Couscous with
Raisins, Pine Nuts, and
Roasted Shallots

BEAN AND CAULIFLOWER PURÉE

Cauliflower provides the sturdy base, but the beans add a richness that makes this dish. You can substitute other white beans such as white kidneys, but if at all possible, get your hands on delicious and rich cannellini beans. Some simple herbs, a little garlic, and high-quality olive oil are just about all you need to round out this lovely dip—perfect with sturdy chips, crusty country bread, fresh-cut veggies, or toasted pita triangles.

1. In a large saucepan over medium-high heat, combine the cauliflower, onion, and garlic. Cover the vegetables with cold water to an inch above their tops. Bring to a boil over medium-high heat. Lightly salt, and cook until the cauliflower is very soft, about 15 minutes. Drain the vegetables, reserving about ½ cup of the cooking liquid.

2. Combine the cooked vegetables with the olive oil, beans, rosemary, and thyme in the bowl of a food processor. Pulse until the vegetables are coarsely chopped. Then leave the processor running until the purée is smooth.

3. Add the cooking liquid, 1 tablespoon at a time, as necessary to create a smooth but thick texture. Season with salt and pepper to taste. Serve warm.

NUTRITIONAL INFORMATION Per Serving: 157 cal., 4 g fat, 1 g sat. fat, 24 g carb., 8 g protein, 426 mg sodium, 1 g sugar, 6 g fiber.

SERVES 4

½ head cauliflower, chopped

½ small yellow onion, chopped

1 clove garlic, smashed

Salt and freshly ground black pepper, to taste

1 tablespoon extra-virgin olive oil

One 14-ounce can cannellini beans, drained

¼ teaspoon dried rosemary

¼ teaspoon dried thyme

WHOLE-WHEAT FUSILLI

WITH 5-MINUTE TOMATO SAUCE

If you're going to capture all the elemental Italian flavors—olive oil, garlic, tomatoes, and parmesan—in a delectable sauce, you might as well pair that sauce with a corkscrew-shaped pasta that has maximum surface area to catch every last drop. This a simple dish, quick and easy to make, but truly gratifying to eat. Whole-wheat pasta ups the vitamin and antioxidants, fiber and protein . . . but the hearty flavor and texture are the real sell.

SERVES 4

12 ounces whole-wheat fusilli (or substitute whole-grain fusilli)

One 28-ounce can reduced-sodium whole peeled tomatoes

1 large clove garlic, smashed

Salt and freshly ground black pepper, to taste

½ tablespoon extra-virgin olive oil

2 teaspoons balsamic vinegar

12 large fresh basil leaves, thinly sliced

3 teaspoons grated low-sodium parmesan, for serving

1. Bring a large pot of heavily salted water to a boil. Cook the pasta according to the package instructions.

2. While the pasta cooks, combine the tomatoes and garlic in the bowl of a food processor and pulse until finely chopped. Transfer to a large mixing bowl. Add the olive oil, vinegar, and basil, and mix well. Season with salt and pepper to taste.

3. Drain the pasta thoroughly, and then add the hot pasta to the sauce in the mixing bowl. Transfer to a serving bowl and sprinkle with the parmesan. Serve warm.

NUTRITIONAL INFORMATION Per Serving: 377 cal., 7 g fat, 1 g sat. fat, 68 g carb., 17 g protein, 199 mg sodium, 5 g sugar, 9 g fiber.

Whole-Wheat Fusilli
with 5-Minute
Tomato Sauce

ROASTED BROCCOLINI WITH GARLIC AND CHILES

If you've never tried broccolini, there's no better opportunity to get acquainted with this interesting and flavor-packed vegetable than this dish. A cross between broccoli and Chinese kale, broccolini is chock-full of nutrients, including vitamin C, folate, iron, and calcium. The robust flavor is closer to asparagus than to broccoli, but is a treat regardless. With just a little sharpness courtesy of chili flakes and lemon, the vegetable shines as a side dish or a quick, nutritious snack.

SERVES 4

2 bunches broccolini (about 1½ pounds), trimmed

3 cloves garlic, thinly sliced lengthwise

2 tablespoons extra-virgin olive oil

Salt and freshly ground black pepper, to taste

½ teaspoon red chili flakes, or to taste

½ lemon

1. Preheat the oven to 400 degrees F.

2. Spread the broccolini on a baking sheet, with the stems facing in the same direction. Scatter the garlic slices over the broccolini and drizzle the olive oil over them. Season with salt and pepper and toss the broccolini until well coated with oil.

3. Roast the broccolini, turning once with tongs. Cook until soft and beginning to char, about 15 minutes total.

4. Arrange the broccolini on a serving platter. Sprinkle with chili flakes. Squeeze lemon juice evenly over the top and serve warm.

NUTRITIONAL INFORMATION Per Serving: 93 cal., 7 g fat, 1 g sat. fat, 4 g carb., 2 g protein, 168 mg sodium, 1 g sugar, 5 g fiber.

Roasted Broccolini with Garlic and Chiles

CRISPY SWEET POTATO WEDGES WITH GINGER-SOY GLAZE

Get ready to give up on traditional baked potatoes. This tasty alternative will also give the boot to home fries, french fries, and just about every other type of crispy potato out there. That's because the potato's delicate sweetness is emphasized by the complex and scintillating combination of ginger and soy sauce. Add a little honey for a sugary sparkle, and you've got just about the best potato-based snack you can make.

SERVES 4

- 2 tablespoons extra-virgin olive oil
- 3 large sweet potatoes, cut lengthwise into ½-inch-thick wedges
- Salt and freshly ground black pepper, to taste
- 1 tablespoon honey
- 1 teaspoon finely grated fresh ginger
- 1 teaspoon low-sodium soy sauce

1. Brush a nonstick baking sheet with 1 tablespoon of the olive oil until evenly coated. Put the pan in the oven and preheat the oven to 400 degrees F.

2. In a large bowl, drizzle the remaining olive oil over the potato wedges and season them with salt and pepper.

3. When the oven and pan are hot, arrange the potato wedges on the pan, cut-side down. Roast until the bottom sides are golden, about 15 minutes. Use tongs to flip the potatoes, and bake until the undersides are brown, 10 to 15 minutes more.

4. While the potatoes bake, combine the honey, ginger, and soy sauce in a small bowl. Whisk until incorporated.

5. Transfer the baked potato wedges to a serving bowl. Drizzle with the honey mixture and gently toss to coat. Serve warm.

NUTRITIONAL INFORMATION Per Serving: 225 cal., 7 g fat, 1 g sat. fat, 37 g carb., 2 g protein, 213 mg sodium, 14 g sugar, 4 g fiber.

Crispy Sweet Potato
Wedges with
Ginger-Soy Glaze

MEXICAN COUSCOUS

Mexican dishes are more commonly served with rice, but couscous offers a way to break up the routine and inject a surprisingly nutty addition to a lovely side dish. A dose of jalapeño pepper adds some south-of-the-border bite to the flavor combinations—and ripe tomatoes, avocado, and cilantro drive home the Mexican roots of the dish. Not surprisingly, this unique creation echoes the most alluring flavors in guacamole.

SERVES 6

2 cups low-sodium chicken stock (or substitute low-sodium vegetable broth)

½ small white onion, chopped

1 small clove garlic, minced

½ small jalapeño pepper, seeded and minced

½ teaspoon salt

Freshly ground black pepper, to taste

½ teaspoon chili powder

One 10-ounce box couscous

2 vine-ripened tomatoes, seeded and diced

¼ cup chopped fresh cilantro

Zest and juice of 1 lime

½ ripe avocado, peeled, pitted and diced

1. In a large saucepan over medium-high heat, combine the stock, onion, garlic, jalapeño, salt, pepper, and chili powder. Bring to a boil and then reduce to a simmer. Cook for about 2 minutes.

2. Place the couscous in a large bowl and pour the liquid over it. Cover tightly with plastic wrap and let stand for 10 minutes.

3. Uncover the bowl and fluff the couscous with a fork. Add the tomatoes, cilantro, lime zest and juice, and the avocado. Stir well to combine. Serve warm or at room temperature.

NUTRITIONAL INFORMATION Per Serving: 215 cal., 7 g fat, 1 g sat. fat, 49 g carb., 9 g protein, 265 mg sodium, 3 g sugar, 5 g fiber.

HERB-ROASTED FINGERLING POTATOES

Fingerlings are a fun departure from other potato varieties, not only because they are naturally bite-sized but also because they come in a variety of colors from traditional yellow to purple. The look will impress dinner guests, but it's the simple, light flavor—helped along by a complement of herbs—that will complete the dinner table. The flavors are tremendously adaptable as well, and the potatoes go perfectly with the heartiest beef, light veal, or even chicken.

1. Put a baking sheet in the oven and preheat the oven to 400 degrees F.

2. In a small bowl, whisk together the olive oil, butter, thyme, rosemary, oregano, and garlic powder until emulsified.

3. In a large bowl, combine the potatoes and dressing and toss until well coated (be sure the cut sides of the potatoes are coated with dressing).

4. Remove the hot pan from the oven and, using tongs, place the potatoes on the cut-side down. Roast until the potato flesh turns golden, about 15 minutes. Turn the potatoes with a spatula and continue roasting until soft when pierced with a knife.

5. Transfer the cooked potatoes to a serving bowl and season with salt and pepper to taste. Serve warm.

NUTRITIONAL INFORMATION Per Serving: 172 cal., 4 g fat, 1 g sat. fat, 30 g carb., 6 g protein, 155 mg sodium, 0 g sugar, 0 g fiber.

SERVES 4

1 tablespoon extra-virgin olive oil

1 tablespoon unsalted butter, melted

¼ teaspoon dried or fresh thyme

¼ teaspoon dried or fresh rosemary

¼ teaspoon dried oregano

¼ teaspoon garlic powder

1½ pounds fingerling potatoes, halved lengthwise

Salt and freshly ground black pepper, to taste

GREEN GODDESS WEDGE SALAD

This is a re-imagining of an old-fashioned steak-house favorite. Plain-as-can-be iceberg lettuce (but with that oh-so-satisfying crunch) serves as the subtle stage for a dynamite dressing that is the real star of this salad. Fresh herbs (which supply the green), tangy buttermilk, and a tiny bit of garlic make for a fun and colorful dressing. It offers a smooth and elegant contrast to the lettuce and pop of the mini-tomatoes scattered on top.

SERVES 4

¼ cup nonfat plain yogurt

⅓ cup low-fat buttermilk

2 tablespoons chopped fresh chives, plus more for garnish

2 tablespoons chopped fresh flat-leaf parsley

¼ teaspoon salt

Freshly ground black pepper, to taste

1 small clove garlic, chopped

1 small head iceberg lettuce, cut into 4 wedges

½ cup cherry or grape tomatoes, halved

Chopped fresh chives, for garnish

1. Combine the yogurt, buttermilk, chives, parsley, salt, pepper, and garlic in the container of a small food processor or blender and purée until smooth.

2. Place the lettuce wedges on 4 salad plates. Drizzle the dressing evenly over the wedges. Top each wedge with a scattering of tomatoes and fresh chives and serve.

NUTRITIONAL INFORMATION Per Serving: 76 cal., 1 g fat, 0 g sat. fat, 12 g carb., 6 g protein, 382 mg sodium, 5 g sugar, 5 g fiber.

Green Goddess
Wedge Salad

SNACKS

6

Herb and White Bean Hummus

Chickpea-Yogurt Dip

Mexican Pita Chips

Simple, Gorgeous Glazed Carrots

Artichoke-Basil Dip

Savory Granola

Mediterranean Popcorn

Feta-Chive–Stuffed Cherry Tomatoes

Sweet and Spicy Pecans

Smoky Kale Chips

Mozzarella-Tomato Skewers

Crackers with Apple-Cinnamon Peanut Butter

Cheese and Olive-Stuffed Cucumbers

Smoked Salmon Pinwheels

Sweet and Spicy Pretzels

Peanut Butter Milk Shakes

Chili-Lime Jicama Sticks

Orange-Almond Pudding

English Muffin Grilled Cheese-and-Apple Wedges

Crunchy Provolone-and-Tomato-Stuffed Mushrooms

Your Bridge Between Meals

Snacking is one of the most important nutritional components of the day. So much attention is paid to meals that snacks always seem to be an afterthought. This is a big mistake when it comes to eating well and maintaining or losing weight. Snacks are bridges between meals and can carry us over troubled waters. Snacks may have a bad rap because many people consume an entire meal's worth of calories in what they think is a snack. With these recipes, you won't fall into that trap.

Snacks are not a mandatory part of the SHRED lifestyle, but they are heavily encouraged. They can prevent you from overindulging at mealtime because they prevent you from becoming so ravenous that you want to eat everything in sight. Smart, strategic snacking can also keep blood sugars stable and hormone levels consistent.

A smart snacker is a smart eater. It's not just about the calories you consume; it's also about what comes with those calories. Snacks that contain protein, fiber, and lots of other nutrients are much better than sugary snacks like doughnuts and cookies that offer no real nutritional value and quickly trigger a sugar crash. Fiber and protein can help fill you up so that you can make it to the next meal without being tempted to eat something that you shouldn't be eating. Crunchy snacks—foods that include nuts, celery, carrots, cucumbers, and the like—help suppress your appetite. Consider snacks a mini-refueling opportunity that can keep you going until you're able to fill up your tank completely.

Pay particular attention to the portion sizes of the snacks as well as their calories, and make choices that fit what is suggested on the SHRED plan you're currently following. Even if you're not following a plan, these snacks can work for you as well. Who says snacks can't be creative, fun, healthy, and low-cal. I hope you immensely enjoy these recipes with all their savory goodness and nutritional power.

HERB AND WHITE BEAN HUMMUS

White beans offer a subtler, more elegant flavor than chickpeas, but provide the same great body that defines a classic hummus. Of course, healthy tahini makes any hummus a hummus, but beyond that, the dip is open to definition. This particular version includes an alluring mix of herbs sprinkled in along with some traditional lemon juice. Add a little minced garlic if you prefer—or even a dash of cayenne pepper if you like things on the hot side.

1. In a small bowl, combine the lemon juice, basil, parsley, chives, thyme, and garlic powder. Let stand for at least 10 minutes.

2. Combine the beans, olive oil, tahini, salt, black pepper, and lemon juice mixture in the bowl of a food processor. Pulse just until thick and chunky.

3. Transfer to a bowl and serve with the pita chips.

NUTRITIONAL INFORMATION Per Serving: 243 cal., 17 g fat, 2 g sat. fat, 34 g carb., 8 g protein, 368 mg sodium, 2 g sugar, 5 g fiber.

SERVES 4 TO 6

2 tablespoons fresh lemon juice

1 teaspoon dried basil

1 teaspoon dried parsley

1 teaspoon dried chives

½ teaspoon dried thyme

¼ teaspoon garlic powder

One 15-ounce can reduced-sodium cannellini or other white bean, drained

3 tablespoons extra-virgin olive oil

2 tablespoons tahini

⅛ teaspoon salt

Freshly ground black pepper, as needed

Baked pita chips (or substitute celery and carrot sticks)

Chickpea-Yogurt Dip

CHICKPEA-YOGURT DIP

With their buttery mouthfeel, pleasingly nutty flavor, and tons of insoluble fiber, chickpeas are just about the perfect dip base. Combine them with the creaminess of Greek yogurt and just a couple of traditional Middle Eastern spices and you have a champion dip for any time—weeknight, movie night, or even a game day spread. The dip is ideal with the pita, especially if it's mildly toasted. Or pair the dip with fresh, crunchy veggies such as celery or jicama.

1. Combine the chickpeas, garlic, lime zest and juice, and olive oil in the bowl of a food processor. Pulse until the mixture is coarse.

2. Add the salt, cumin, and coriander, and pulse to combine. Add the yogurt and purée until very smooth. If the dip is too thick, add a bit more yogurt.

3. Taste the dip and add salt and pepper to taste. Transfer to a serving bowl and sprinkle with chopped cilantro. Serve with the pita torn into pieces.

NUTRITIONAL INFORMATION Per Serving: 242 cal., 8 g fat, 1 g sat. fat, 32 g carb., 11 g protein, 328 mg sodium, 4 g sugar, 5 g fiber.

SERVES 4 TO 6

One 15-ounce can reduced-sodium chickpeas, drained and rinsed

1 clove garlic, chopped

Zest and juice of 1 lime

1 tablespoon extra-virgin olive oil

½ teaspoon salt

¼ teaspoon ground cumin

¼ teaspoon ground coriander

⅓ cup nonfat plain Greek yogurt

Salt and freshly ground black pepper, to taste

Chopped fresh cilantro, for garnish

Whole-wheat pita (or crackers, or celery sticks), for dipping

MEXICAN PITA CHIPS

Let's face it, potato chips are easy and delicious. But you can fight the instant gratification urge by keeping healthy chip alternatives around, and you won't find a better choice than these chips. Baking makes for a much healthier chip than frying, and you don't lose any flavor when you bake a piece of pita. Cover those chips with a dusting of spices and you have an ideal snack for dipping or eating plain.

SERVES 6 TO 8

⅛ teaspoon salt
½ teaspoon ground cumin
½ teaspoon ground coriander
½ teaspoon dried oregano
½ teaspoon chili powder
¼ teaspoon cayenne pepper
3 pitas, plain or whole-wheat
Olive oil cooking spray

1. Preheat the oven to 375 degrees F. Line a baking sheet with parchment paper.

2. In a small bowl, combine the salt, cumin, coriander, oregano, chili powder, and cayenne and stir until combined.

3. Cut each pita into 8 wedges. If the wedges separate easily, pull them apart (the thinner pita pieces will make crispier chips). Arrange the wedges on the baking sheet and spray them with the cooking spray. Sprinkle the chips with half the spice mixture. Flip the wedges over and repeat with the other half of the spice mix.

4. Bake in the center of the oven until light golden and crisp, 12 to 15 minutes. Flip the chips once halfway through cooking. Let the chips cool before serving.

NUTRITIONAL INFORMATION Per Serving: 116 cal., 1 g fat, 0 g sat. fat, 22 g carb., 3 g protein, 209 mg sodium, 1 g sugar, 1 g fiber.

Mexican Pita Chips

SIMPLE, GORGEOUS GLAZED CARROTS

Call it a surprisingly scrumptious nonfat snack, a scintillating side dish, a show-stopping appetizer, or just a wonderful dish in its own right and you'll probably wind up just calling them spectacular. These carrots will impress wherever and whenever they're served. As if the intriguing mix of garden freshness, sweetness, and citrus wasn't enough, the dish is easy and simple to make. It might be right at home in the middle of a special occasion dinner spread, but it's also just the thing to round out a quick, no-fuss weeknight meal.

SERVES 4

6 large carrots, peeled
   and sliced
1 tablespoon dark brown sugar
2 tablespoons orange juice
1 teaspoon honey

1. Fill a large pot three-quarters full of water and bring to a boil over high heat. Add the carrots and cook just until tender enough for a fork to pierce a slice, about 7 minutes.

2. While the carrots are cooking, combine the brown sugar, orange juice, and honey in a small bowl. Whisk to incorporate.

3. Drain the carrots and return them to the pot. Pour the glaze over the carrots and cook on high for about 2 minutes, until the glaze is reduced and thickens. Reduce to a simmer and cook off any extra liquid. Serve the carrots hot.

NUTRITIONAL INFORMATION Per Serving: 52 cal., 0 g fat, 0 g sat. fat, 12 g carb., 2 g protein, 63 mg sodium, 8 g sugar, 3 g fiber.

Simple, Gorgeous
Glazed Carrots

Artichoke-Basil Dip

ARTICHOKE-BASIL DIP

Here's a last-minute party treat that will fill the bill for a cookout snack table, a dip for the big game, or just something to spread on a quick and satisfying sandwich. Artichoke is most often paired with spinach in a dip. This combination is a bit more refined, a little sweeter and more interesting. The parmesan adds a bit of cheesy goodness, making the dip seem a bit decadent without going over the top of calories or fat.

Combine all the ingredients in the bowl of a food processor and pulse until nearly smooth. Season with salt and pepper to taste.

NUTRITIONAL INFORMATION Per Serving: 52 cal., 3 g fat, 0 g sat. fat, 3 g carb., 2 g protein, 248 mg sodium, 1 g sugar, 4 g fiber.

**SERVES 4 TO 6
(ABOUT 1 1/2 CUPS)**

One 14-ounce can artichoke hearts in water, drained and halved

2 tablespoons finely grated parmesan

1 tablespoon extra-virgin olive oil

2 teaspoons white wine vinegar

12 large fresh basil leaves, chopped

Salt and freshly ground black pepper, to taste

SAVORY GRANOLA

Sometimes sweet won't cut it. When you need a snack that is savory and complex—a little more late afternoon than early morning—try this granola. It packs a big nutrition punch with loads of healthy fats, usable calories, and valuable fiber. More importantly, it stops hunger pangs in their tracks with the filling goodness of nuts, oats, and slightly spicy seasonings. As snacks go, this one puts potato chips to shame.

SERVES 8

1 cup old-fashioned rolled oats

½ cup whole almonds

½ cup pecan halves

½ cup unsalted peanuts

½ cup raw, unsalted sunflower seeds

1 large egg white, beaten until foamy

1 tablespoon canola oil

½ teaspoon Worcestershire sauce

¼ teaspoon ground cumin

Pinch garlic powder

Pinch cayenne pepper

Salt and freshly ground pepper, to taste

1. Preheat the oven to 325 degrees F. Line a baking sheet with parchment paper.

2. Combine the oats, almonds, pecans, peanuts, and sunflower seeds in a medium mixing bowl.

3. In a small bowl, whisk together the egg white, canola oil, Worcestershire sauce, cumin, garlic powder, cayenne, salt, and pepper until combined and frothy. Pour the mixture over the dry mix and toss well to coat evenly.

4. Spread the mixture in an even single layer on the baking sheet. Bake, stirring once halfway through, until light golden brown, 25 to 30 minutes.

5. Cool the granola on the pan and break up any large clumps. Eat when cool, or store in an airtight container.

NUTRITIONAL INFORMATION Per Serving: 231 cal., 34 g fat, 2 g sat. fat, 14 g carb., 11 g protein, 104 mg sodium, 2 g sugar, 5 g fiber.

Savory
Granola

MEDITERRANEAN POPCORN

As snacks go, it's awfully hard to beat popcorn for a filling, quick hunger killer. Although popcorn itself is incredibly light and insubstantial, it is also surprisingly filling. This particular version of the movie-house standard foregoes the butter, opting instead for flavor fireworks courtesy of a spice mix that would make a Greek chef proud. A little parmesan adds just a hint of fat, but otherwise the modest calories make this a completely guilt-free snack.

SERVES 6 TO 8 (ABOUT 8 CUPS)

¼ cup grated parmesan

Zest of 1 lemon

½ teaspoon dried oregano

¼ teaspoon dried thyme

Pinch of garlic powder

1 cup air-popped popcorn, warm

2 tablespoons extra-virgin
   olive oil

Salt and freshly ground black
   pepper, to taste

1. In a small bowl, combine the parmesan, lemon zest, oregano, thyme, and garlic powder. Stir to mix.

2. Put the warm popcorn in a serving bowl. Drizzle half of the olive oil over it and toss. Repeat with the remaining olive oil and toss well.

3. Sprinkle about half of the cheese mixture over the popcorn. Season lightly with salt and pepper to taste and toss. Repeat with the remaining cheese mixture, and toss until thoroughly mixed. Serve with napkins!

NUTRITIONAL INFORMATION Per Serving: 19 cal., 1.2 g fat, 0 g sat. fat, 1g carb., 1 g protein, 195 mg sodium, 0 g sugar, 0 g fiber.

FETA-CHIVE-STUFFED CHERRY TOMATOES

The best snacks are fun finger food, easy to eat as well as delicious. These little gems fit that description and then some. Essentially miniature beefsteaks, cherry tomatoes are a delightful way to get your vitamin C, along with a nice bit of fiber and protein. But it's the irresistible combination of salty feta and fresh tomato flavor that will ultimately draw you in. It's a perfect snack, and a great tray-filler for your next party!

1. In a small bowl, combine the cheese, chives, olive oil, and pepper. Mash with a fork to mix.

2. Use a small serrated knife to slice through the top third of each tomato. Scoop out the seeds with a small spoon.

3. Stuff about 1 teaspoon of the feta cheese mixture into each tomato and set them upright on a plate. Serve immediately or refrigerate for up to 8 hours.

NUTRITIONAL INFORMATION Per Serving: 110 cal., 10 g fat, 3 g sat. fat, 4g carb., 2 g protein, 164 mg sodium, 1 g sugar, 0 g fiber.

SERVES 4

2 ounces crumbled feta cheese

1 tablespoon chopped fresh chives

1 teaspoon extra-virgin olive oil

Freshly ground black pepper, to taste

12 large cherry tomatoes

Sweet and
Spicy Pecans

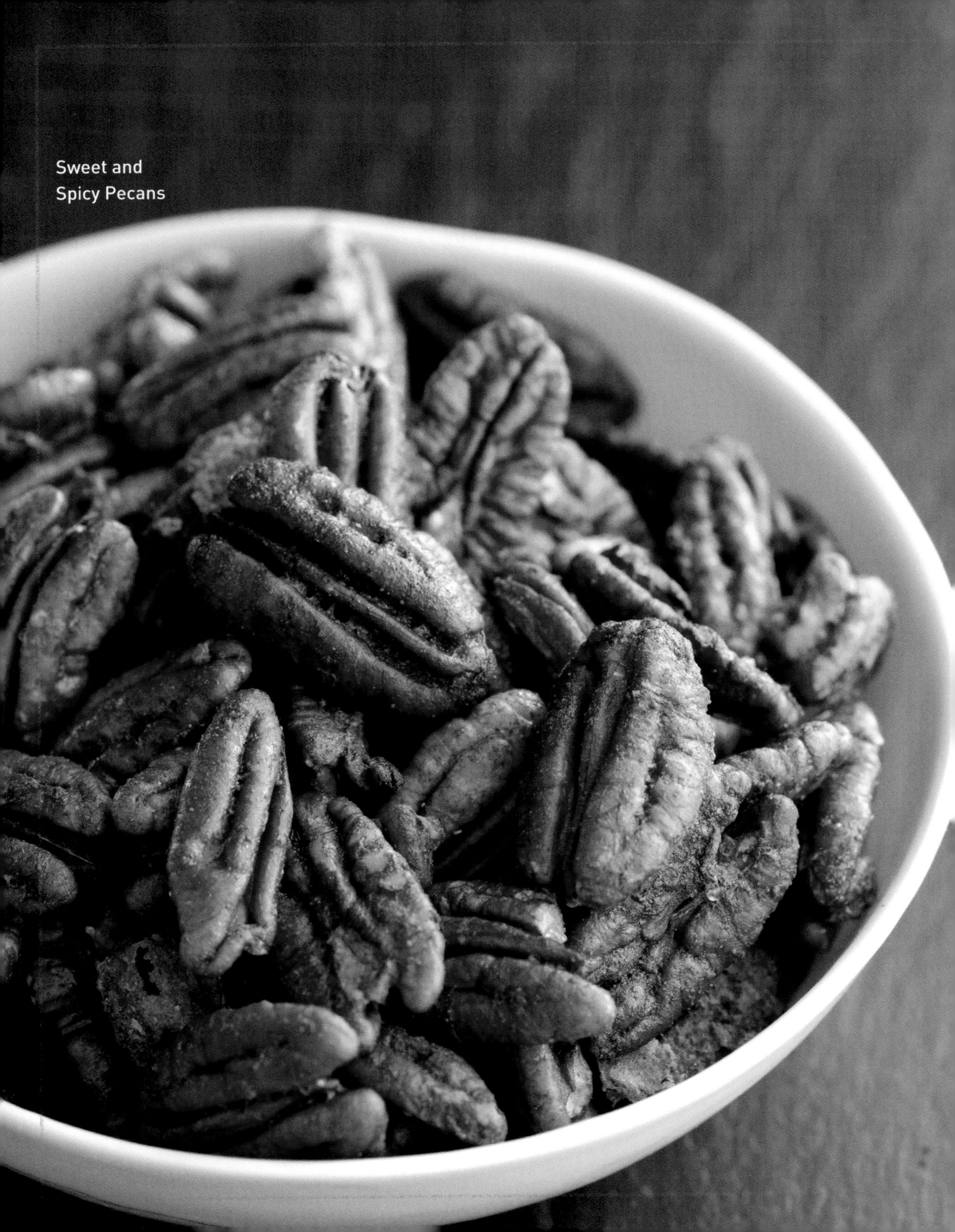

SWEET AND SPICY PECANS

This tasty snack captures the attraction of pralines with a sturdier flavor mix that includes the savory with the sweet. They are no slouch in the health department either. Pecans are packed with some of the highest antioxidant levels of any nut, making this snack as heart-healthy as it is flavorful. It's also a quick hit of nutrition, a fantastic snack to eat whenever your energy is lagging or hunger gets the better of you between meals.

1. Preheat the oven to 300 degrees F. Line a baking sheet with parchment paper.

2. Place the pecans in a mixing bowl. In another bowl, combine the egg white, honey, salt, cinnamon, ginger, and cayenne and beat until foamy and lightened.

3. Pour the egg white mixture over the nuts and toss until evenly coated. Pour the nuts onto the lined baking sheet and spread them out into an even, single layer.

4. Bake, stirring occasionally, until golden brown and crisp, about 30 minutes. Cool completely on the pan and then eat or store in an airtight container.

NUTRITIONAL INFORMATION Per Serving: 142 cal., 25 g fat, 2 g sat. fat, 5 g carb., 4 g protein, 166 mg sodium, 2 g sugar, 3 g fiber.

SERVES 4 TO 6 (ABOUT 2 CUPS)

1¼ cups pecan halves

1 large egg white, beaten

1 tablespoon honey

½ teaspoon salt

¼ teaspoon ground cinnamon

¼ teaspoon ground ginger

¼ teaspoon cayenne pepper

SMOKY KALE CHIPS

Who needs potato chips, when the king of super-foods makes for a tasty, nutrition-packed chip that's best homemade? These chips could not be easier to make or more guilt-free to eat. That's because when you bake them as in this recipe, you lock in the treasure trove of nutrients that this leafy green contains. Dust these chips with a little smoked paprika and they become the richer cousin to barbecue-flavored potato chips. Eat them by the handful—they are amazingly low-cal!

SERVES 4

1 large bunch kale, stems removed and leaves torn in half

½ teaspoon salt

½ teaspoon smoked paprika

Freshly ground black pepper, to taste

Olive oil cooking spray

1. Preheat the oven to 250 degrees F.

2. Spread the kale leaves in a single layer on a large baking sheet. In a small bowl, combine the salt, paprika, and pepper and stir to mix.

3. Lightly spray the surface of the leaves with cooking spray and sprinkle half of the seasoned salt mixture evenly over them. Turn them over, spray again, and sprinkle the rest of the seasoned salt mixture over the leaves.

4. Bake until crisp, about 30 minutes. Cool completely before storing in an airtight container at room temperature.

NUTRITIONAL INFORMATION Per Serving: 36 cal., 1 g fat, 0 g sat. fat, 7 g carb., 2 g protein, 184 mg sodium, 0 g sugar, 1 g fiber.

Smoky Kale
Chips

MOZZARELLA-TOMATO SKEWERS

Mozzarella and tomatoes naturally go hand-in-hand and are the basis of one of the simplest and most delicious of Italian salads, the classic insalata caprese. This snack takes its cue from that wonderful combination, using miniature tomatoes and mozzarella balls that are combined in a portable single serving. The flavors are all simple, fresh, and luscious, and this particular edible could not be more convenient—it's even perfect as a self-contained grab-and-go treat!

SERVES 4

24 small cherry tomatoes

16 mini mozzarella balls (*bocconcini*)

1 tablespoon extra-virgin olive oil

Salt and freshly ground black pepper

⅓ cup grated parmesan

Zest of ½ lemon

1. Thread eight 8-inch wooden skewers with 3 cherry tomatoes and 2 mozzarella balls each. Drizzle olive oil over the skewers, turning them to lightly coat. Season each with salt and pepper.

2. Pour the parmesan onto a shallow plate and scatter the lemon zest over it. Dip each skewer into the parmesan, rolling to coat, and serve. These can be made up to an hour ahead of time.

NUTRITIONAL INFORMATION Per Serving: 170 cal., 14 g fat, 6 g sat. fat, 6 g carb., 8 g protein, 203 mg sodium, 3 g sugar, 1 g fiber.

CRACKERS WITH APPLE-CINNAMON PEANUT BUTTER

These are little one-bite delights meant to stave off hunger and keep you going without slowing you down. There are many different kinds of whole-wheat crackers you can use to make these; choose the flattest, sturdiest you can find. It's also worth the modest added cost to buy organic applesauce; not only is the flavor richer, but you'll be cutting out any unneeded additives.

In a small bowl, combine the peanut butter, applesauce, and cinnamon and stir to mix. Spread about 1½ teaspoons of the mixture on each cracker and serve.

NUTRITIONAL INFORMATION Per Serving: 182 cal., 12 g fat, 1 g sat. fat, 16 g carb., 4 g protein, 150 mg sodium, 1 g sugar, 2 g fiber.

SERVES 4

¼ cup natural crunchy peanut butter

2 tablespoons applesauce

½ teaspoon ground cinnamon

12 whole-wheat crackers

CHEESE-AND-OLIVE-STUFFED CUCUMBERS

Kalamata olives lend their savory bite to the filling in these cucumbers and chives and pepper round out the flavors. It's a simple snack, but one that creates a lot of interest by playing the clean, lightly sweet cucumber against the smooth and rich cream cheese. These take very little time and effort to make but are elegant and fun enough to serve at a cocktail party. The minimal calories mean you can safely feast on a large handful.

SERVES 4

1 English cucumber, cut into
   12 equal slices

2 ounces (about ¼ cup) low-fat
   cream cheese

8 pitted Kalamata olives, finely
   chopped

½ teaspoon dried chives

Freshly ground black pepper,
   to taste

1. Arrange the cucumber slices on a serving plate. Use a melon baller or small spoon to dig out the center of each cucumber slice without cutting all of the way through.

2. In a small bowl, mash the cream cheese, olives, chives, and black pepper with a fork until thoroughly combined.

3. Transfer the mixture to a small resealable plastic bag. Snip off one corner, and squeeze about 1 teaspoon of the cream cheese mixture into each cucumber cup. Serve immediately.

NUTRITIONAL INFORMATION Per Serving: 51 cal., 3 g fat, 2 g sat. fat, 3 g carb., 2 g protein, 186 mg sodium, 2 g sugar, 1 g fiber.

SMOKED SALMON PINWHEELS

Classic taste sensations often make the best snacks because interesting flavors make up for small quantities of food. These lovely little beauties trade on the salty richness and sweet creaminess of lox and cream cheese, but in a form with far fewer calories and fat than the traditional bagel topping. These are a great make-ahead treat that can be pulled out of the refrigerator at a moment's notice.

1. Spread the cream cheese over the surface of the tortilla. Sprinkle the dill and chopped capers evenly across the layer of cream cheese.

2. Lay the salmon on top in an even, single layer. Roll the tortilla up into a tight cylinder. Wrap tightly in plastic wrap and refrigerate until ready to serve.

3. To serve, slice the tortilla roll crosswise with a serrated knife into 12 equal slices.

NUTRITIONAL INFORMATION Per Serving: 101 cal., 3 g fat, 1 g sat. fat, 13 g carb., 5 g protein, 339 mg sodium, 0 g sugar, 2 g fiber.

SERVES 4

One 12-inch whole-wheat tortilla

2 tablespoons whipped low-fat cream cheese

½ teaspoon dried dill

1 teaspoon brined capers, drained and chopped

2 ounces smoked salmon

SWEET AND SPICY PRETZELS

The best snacks offer something for every part of the palate, and these pretzels fill that bill in a big way. The recipe cuts down on the sodium by using unsalted pretzels, but the spice mix provides all the saltiness that your tongue needs. Along the way, it adds the simple sweetness of brown sugar and savory spice.

SERVES 4

1 teaspoon olive oil

1 teaspoon packed light brown sugar

¼ teaspoon cinnamon

¼ teaspoon ground ginger

¼ teaspoon cayenne pepper

Pinch salt (if needed)

2 cups unsalted mini pretzels (if you can't find them, use salted and omit salt in step 2)

1. Preheat the oven to 350 degrees F. Line a baking sheet with parchment paper.

2. In a small bowl, whisk together the olive oil, brown sugar, cinnamon, ginger, cayenne, and salt (if using unsalted pretzels) until combined. Add the pretzels to a large bowl and drizzle half of the sweet and spicy mixture over the pretzels. Toss vigorously to coat. Drizzle the remaining sweet and spicy mixture over the pretzels, mix well, and spread them out in an even layer on the baking sheet.

3. Bake until crisp and hot, about 10 minutes. Cool to room temperature before serving.

NUTRITIONAL INFORMATION Per Serving: 97 cal., 1 g fat, 0 g sat. fat, 20 g carb., 2 g protein, 211 mg sodium, 3 g sugar, 1 g fiber.

PEANUT BUTTER MILK SHAKES

Almond milk is just right to smooth out the peanut butter richness of this fun, fast, and fantastic liquid snack. Although this is just about as decadent-tasting as a snack can get, the sugar in this shake is unprocessed and restrained. The flavor comes from the combination of a bananas and peanut butter, and it's an even better combination than peanut butter and chocolate. You'll get a big energy boost from this one, and kids love it too.

Combine all the ingredients in the canister of a blender and purée until smooth. Pour into 4 glasses and enjoy!

NUTRITIONAL INFORMATION Per Serving: 162 cal., 9 g fat, 1 g sat. fat, 15 g carb., 4 g protein, 133 mg sodium, 9 g sugar, 2 g fiber.

SERVES 4

1 ripe banana, sliced

¼ cup natural creamy peanut butter

2 cups vanilla light almond milk

2 teaspoons honey

CHILI-LIME JICAMA STICKS

You simply won't find a better potato chip alternative. Jicama combines the best of many other vegetables and fruits—the clean crispness of a Granny Smith apple, the firmness of a potato, and the moist snap of just-picked celery—all with a distinctive, understated radish-like flavor. Add a little zip with some citrus and spice and you have the makings of a tongue-tingling midday wake-up call that will leave you ready to tackle whatever comes next.

SERVES 4

1 large jicama, peeled and cut into ¼-inch-wide sticks
Juice of ½ lime
½ teaspoon salt
½ teaspoon sugar
½ teaspoon chili powder
Zest of 1 lime

1. Spread the jicama on a shallow plate. Distribute the lime juice over the sticks to moisten.

2. In a small bowl, combine the salt, sugar, and chili powder and stir to mix. Sprinkle the mixture over the jicama sticks. Toss to coat.

3. Sprinkle the lime zest over the top and serve.

NUTRITIONAL INFORMATION Per Serving: 67 cal., 0 g fat, 0 g sat. fat, 16 g carb., 1 g protein, 297 mg sodium, 4 g sugar, 8 g fiber.

ORANGE-ALMOND PUDDING

Plain old pudding has its fond place in childhood memories, but when looking to fill the blank space between two meals, you'll want a memorable pudding. Look no further. A delicate dance of almond and orange make this concoction smooth and distinctive. Every spoonful has just the right balance of fruity sweetness and savory nuttiness. It's time to make some new culinary memories!

1. In a medium bowl, combine the pudding mix, almond milk, and almond extract. Whisk for 2 minutes until very smooth and beginning to thicken.

2. Divide the orange segments among 4 wide juice glasses and fill each glass with one-quarter of the pudding mixture. Refrigerate until firm.

3. Sprinkle 1 tablespoon of almonds on top of each pudding before serving.

NUTRITIONAL INFORMATION Per Serving: 87 cal., 4 g fat, 0 g sat. fat, 13 g carb., 2 g protein, 95 mg sodium, 8 g sugar, 2 g fiber.

SERVES 4

One 1-ounce package sugar-free vanilla instant pudding

2 cups light almond milk

3 drops almond extract

One 11-ounce can mandarin orange segments, drained

¼ cup sliced almonds, toasted

ENGLISH MUFFIN GRILLED CHEESE-AND-APPLE WEDGES

This quick snack puts an interesting twist on both the classic grilled cheese sandwich and the time-tested combo of cheddar and apple. Melt cheese on an English muffin and it's like filling a rugged landscape with comforting and gooey deliciousness. Melt two cheeses on the muffin and you double the perfection. Add fresh apple slices to all that and you inject a pop of crunchy tartness that brings everything together in one fiber-rich package.

SERVES 4

Olive oil cooking spray

2 whole-grain English muffins, split

2 thin slices cheddar cheese

½ Granny Smith apple, peeled, cored, and very thinly sliced

2 thin slices provolone

1. Coat a medium nonstick skillet with olive oil cooking spray and heat it over medium-low heat.

2. Top each muffin bottom with a slice of cheddar cheese. Layer apple slices on each slice. Top the apples with a slice of provolone and cover with the muffin top.

3. Toast the sandwiches until the bottom turns golden and the cheeses begin to melt, about 5 minutes.

4. Spray the muffin tops with cooking spray and flip the sandwiches in the pan. Lay a sheet of parchment paper over the sandwiches and rest a large, flat skillet on top to weigh down the muffins. Cook until the bottoms turn crisp and golden and the cheeses completely melt, about 5 minutes.

5. Transfer the sandwiches to a cutting board and let stand for 5 minutes. Use a serrated knife to slice each sandwich into six wedges and serve.

NUTRITIONAL INFORMATION Per Serving: 181 cal., 9 g fat, 6 g sat. fat, 25 g carb., 9 g protein, 320 mg sodium, 3 g sugar, 4 g fiber.

Crunchy Provolone-
and-Tomato-Stuffed
Mushrooms

CRUNCHY PROVOLONE-AND-TOMATO-STUFFED MUSHROOMS

Great snacks rely on contrasts to keep your interest—contrasts like the crackly crunch of the filling in this mushroom and the deliciously soft and yielding mushroom texture itself. These bite-sized gems definitely bring strong Italian flavors including traditional spices, intense sun-dried tomatoes, and the tangy melted provolone. Panko breadcrumbs bring all those flavors together in a winning snack symphony.

1. Preheat the oven to 450 degrees F. Line a quarter baking sheet with parchment paper.

2. Use a spoon to hollow out the mushroom caps. Place them top-down on the baking sheet and season with salt and pepper. Roast until soft, about 15 minutes.

3. While the mushrooms roast, combine the breadcrumbs, Italian seasoning, and olive oil in a small bowl. Stir until evenly mixed and moistened.

4. Remove the mushrooms from the oven. Lay one sundried tomato into each cap, followed by a cube of cheese. Sprinkle the breadcrumb mixture into each mushroom cap and return the pan to the oven.

5. Bake until the cheese melts and the breadcrumbs turn golden and crisp, 8 to 10 minutes. Remove and let the mushrooms cool for at least 5 minutes before serving.

NUTRITIONAL INFORMATION Per Serving: 97 cal., 5 g fat, 3 g sat. fat, 8 g carb., 6 g protein, 370 mg sodium, 2 g sugar, 1 g fiber.

SERVES 4

8 large cremini mushrooms, stems removed

Salt and freshly ground black pepper, to taste

¼ cup whole-wheat panko

¼ teaspoon Italian seasoning

1 teaspoon extra-virgin olive oil

8 oil-packed sun-dried tomatoes, drained

2 ounces aged provolone, cut into 8 equal-sized cubes

SMOOTHIES

7

Orange-Burst Smoothie

Exotic Tropical Smoothie

Bodacious Berry Bonanza Smoothie

Vigorous Green Smoothie

Berry Orange Smoothie

Crazy Coconut Smoothie

Stinger Smoothie

Pixilating Pineapple Smoothie

Fun, Filling, Fiber Smoothie

Blueberry-Banana Smoothie

Sweet Kale Energizer Smoothie

Sweet Antioxidant Supreme Smoothie

Sweet Ferocious Fiber Smoothie

Great Green-Grape Smoothie

Ritzy Raspberry Smoothie

Black-and-Blue Twister Smoothie

Papaya-Mango Chiller Smoothie

Raw Green Machine Smoothie

Tropical Twister Smoothie

Sweet Protein-Boost Smoothie

Chia Power Smoothie

Vitamin-C Boost Smoothie

Declan's Simple Morning-Delight Smoothie

Sweet-and-Hearty Oatmeal Smoothie

Watermelon Spritzer Smoothie

Avocado-Pear Blitz Smoothie

Bloody Mary Wake-up Smoothie

Chocolate and Strawberry Smoothie

Super Green Smoothie

Dash's Berry Blast Smoothie

There's no better way to start your day than with a smoothie. Easy, quick, full of vitamins, minerals, and other nutrients, they can be a great start to the day. Smoothies, however, are extremely versatile. You can have them at any time and they still taste great and can serve an important function. Smoothies are all about energy. You could start your morning with something like the Sweet Kale Energizer (page 310) and get an energy pick-me-up in the middle of the day with the Bodacious Berry Bonanza (page 301). Smoothies such as the Fun, Filling, Fiber (page 308) can also be a great meal replacement, helping you save calories yet still deliver a tremendous nutritious punch.

One of my favorite aspects of smoothies is that you can be extremely creative with the recipes. You can exchange ingredients such as raspberries for strawberries. You can choose frozen fruits instead of fresh. You can use light almond milk instead of low-fat milk. Smoothies are built to be customized to your taste preferences and are fun to make. Enjoy these simple recipes and feel free to collaborate with your family. Smoothies are something the entire family can enjoy.

ORANGE-BURST SMOOTHIE

Combine all ingredients in a blender and purée until smooth.

NUTRITIONAL INFORMATION Per Serving: 177 cal., 1 g fat, 1 g sat. fat, 41 g carb., 6 g protein, 41 mg sodium, 34 g sugar, 5 g fiber.

SERVES 2

2 large oranges, peeled and segmented

½ cup frozen peaches

½ ripe banana, peeled and sliced

½ cup low-fat vanilla yogurt

4 ice cubes

BODACIOUS BERRY BONANZA SMOOTHIE

SERVES 2

½ cup frozen blackberries

½ cup frozen blueberries

½ cup frozen raspberries

½ cup frozen strawberries

½ cup low-fat vanilla yogurt

½ cup apple juice (not from concentrate)

Combine all ingredients in a blender and purée until smooth.

NUTRITIONAL INFORMATION Per Serving: 150 cal., 1 g fat, 1 g sat. fat, 33 g carb., 4 g protein, 42 mg sodium, 25 g sugar, 6 g fiber.

Dr. Ian and Alex Martinez prepare the Bodacious Berry Bonanza Smoothie

EXOTIC TROPICAL SMOOTHIE

SERVES 2

½ large mango, peeled, seeded, and chopped

½ papaya, peeled and sliced

½ small kiwi, peeled and sliced

½ cup blueberries

½ cup low-fat vanilla yogurt

1 cup fresh orange juice

6 ice cubes

Combine all ingredients in a blender and purée until smooth.

NUTRITIONAL INFORMATION Per Serving: 203 cal., 1 g fat, 1 g sat. fat, 46 g carb., 5 g protein, 45 mg sodium, 37 g sugar, 4 g fiber.

VIGOROUS GREEN SMOOTHIE

Combine all ingredients in a blender and purée until smooth.

NUTRITIONAL INFORMATION Per Serving: 152 cal., 1 g fat, 1 g sat. fat, 3 g carb., 6 g protein, 121 mg sodium, 20 g sugar, 6 g fiber.

SERVES 2

1 cup chopped kale (stems removed)

1 Granny Smith apple, chopped

1 small ripe banana, peeled and sliced

½ cup low-fat plain yogurt

½ cup coconut water

6 ice cubes

BERRY ORANGE SMOOTHIE

SERVES 2

2 large oranges, peeled, pith removed, chopped

½ cup frozen blueberries

½ cup frozen raspberries

½ cup frozen strawberries

6 ice cubes

Combine all ingredients in a blender and purée until smooth.

NUTRITIONAL INFORMATION Per Serving: 134 cal., 1 g fat, 0 g sat. fat, 34 g carb., 3 g protein, 0 mg sodium, 23 g sugar, 8 g fiber.

CRAZY COCONUT SMOOTHIE

Combine all ingredients in a blender and purée until smooth.

NUTRITIONAL INFORMATION Per Serving: 158 cal., 7 g fat, 6 g sat. fat, 25 g carb., 3 g protein, 67 mg sodium, 10 g sugar, 4 g fiber.

SERVES 2

¾ cup frozen pineapple chunks

1 small ripe banana, peeled and sliced

¼ cup shredded unsweetened coconut

½ cup coconut water

STINGER SMOOTHIE

SERVES 2

½ cup sliced Honeycrisp apples

½ cup frozen strawberries

½ small ripe banana

½ cup low-fat milk (or substitute soy milk)

1 tablespoon bee pollen

4 ice cubes

Combine all ingredients in a blender and purée until smooth.

NUTRITIONAL INFORMATION Per Serving: 84 cal., 1 g fat, 0 g sat. fat, 19 g carb., 2 g protein, 23 mg sodium, 11 g sugar, 3 g fiber.

PIXILATING PINEAPPLE SMOOTHIE

Combine all ingredients in a blender and purée until smooth.

NUTRITIONAL INFORMATION Per Serving: 183 cal., 4 g fat, 2 g sat. fat, 28 g carb., 19 g protein, 73 mg sodium, 27 g sugar, 6 g fiber.

SERVES 2

¾ cup frozen pineapple chunks

⅓ cup diced ripe plums (about 2 small plums)

¼ cup low-fat plain yogurt

¼ cup apple juice (not from concentrate)

¼ cup whey protein powder

FUN, FILLING, FIBER SMOOTHIE

SERVES 2

½ cup beet greens

½ cup sliced apples

½ cup sliced pears

½ cup low-fat blueberry Greek yogurt

½ cup orange juice (not from concentrate)

4 ice cubes

Combine all ingredients in a blender and purée until smooth.

NUTRITIONAL INFORMATION Per Serving: 124 cal., 1 g fat, 0 g sat. fat, 26 g carb., 3 g protein, 74 mg sodium, 22 g sugar, 2 g fiber.

BLUEBERRY-BANANA SMOOTHIE

Combine all ingredients in a blender and purée until smooth.

NUTRITIONAL INFORMATION Per Serving: 136 cal., 3 g fat, 1 g sat. fat, 23 g carb., 6 g protein, 70 mg sodium, 17 g sugar, 3 g fiber.

SERVES 2

1 small ripe banana, peeled and sliced

½ cup frozen blueberries

½ cup low-fat plain yogurt

½ cup low-fat milk (or substitute soy or almond milk)

½ teaspoon flaxseed oil

SWEET KALE ENERGIZER SMOOTHIE

SERVES 2

1 leaf kale, stem removed

½ cup frozen peaches

½ cup frozen mixed berries

½ cup apple cider or apple juice (not from concentrate)

½ teaspoon flaxseed oil

Combine all ingredients in a blender and purée until smooth.

NUTRITIONAL INFORMATION Per Serving: 80 cal., 0 g fat, 0 g sat. fat, 19 g carb., 2 g protein, 0 mg sodium, 16 g sugar, 3 g fiber.

SWEET ANTIOXIDANT SUPREME SMOOTHIE

Combine all ingredients in a blender and purée until smooth.

NUTRITIONAL INFORMATION Per Serving: 103 cal., 0 g fat, 0 g sat. fat, 25 g carb., 2 g protein, 0 mg sodium, 18 g sugar, 3 g fiber.

SERVES 2

½ cup frozen blueberries

½ cup frozen cherries

½ cup frozen strawberries

½ small ripe banana, peeled and sliced

½ cup orange juice (not from concentrate)

4 ice cubes

SWEET FEROCIOUS FIBER SMOOTHIE

SERVES 2

1½ cups red or green pears

½ cup frozen blueberries

½ cup frozen strawberries

½ cup low-fat plain yogurt

½ cup apple juice (not from concentrate)

Combine all ingredients in a blender and purée until smooth.

NUTRITIONAL INFORMATION Per Serving: 166 cal., 1 g fat, 1 g sat. fat, 38 g carb., 4 g protein, 0 mg sodium, 27 g sugar, 6 g fiber.

GREAT GREEN-GRAPE SMOOTHIE

Combine all ingredients in a blender and purée until smooth.

NUTRITIONAL INFORMATION Per Serving: 193 cal., 1 g fat, 1 g sat. fat, 44 g carb., 5 g protein, 48 mg sodium, 36 g sugar, 2 g fiber.

SERVES 2

2 cups frozen green grapes

½ small ripe banana, peeled and sliced

½ cup low-fat plain yogurt

½ cup apple juice (not from concentrate)

RITZY RASPBERRY SMOOTHIE

SERVES 2

½ cup frozen raspberries

½ small ripe banana, peeled and sliced

½ cup low-fat raspberry yogurt

½ cup apple juice (not from concentrate)

½ teaspoon flaxseed oil

Combine all ingredients in a blender and purée until smooth.

NUTRITIONAL INFORMATION Per Serving: 131 cal., 2 g fat, 1 g sat. fat, 26 g carb., 3 g protein, 37 mg sodium, 20 g sugar, 4 g fiber.

BLACK-AND-BLUE TWISTER SMOOTHIE

Combine all ingredients in a blender and purée until smooth.

NUTRITIONAL INFORMATION Per Serving: 125 cal., 1 g fat, 1 g sat. fat, 26 g carb., 5 g protein, 45 mg sodium, 19 g sugar, 4 g fiber.

SERVES 2

½ cup blackberries

½ cup blueberries

½ small ripe banana, peeled and sliced

½ cup low-fat plain yogurt

½ cup apple juice (not from concentrate)

PAPAYA-MANGO CHILLER SMOOTHIE

SERVES 2

1 cup chopped fresh mango

1 cup chopped fresh papaya

½ small ripe banana, peeled and sliced

2 tablespoons fresh lemon juice

6 ice cubes

Combine all ingredients in a blender and purée until smooth.

NUTRITIONAL INFORMATION Per Serving: 107 cal., 0 g fat, 0 g sat. fat, 28 g carb., 2 g protein, 4 mg sodium, 19 g sugar, 4 g fiber.

TROPICAL TWISTER SMOOTHIE

Combine all ingredients in a blender and purée until smooth.

NUTRITIONAL INFORMATION Per Serving: 69 cal., 0 g fat, 0 g sat. fat, 17 g carb., 2 g protein, 70 mg sodium, 10 g sugar, 3 g fiber.

SERVES 2

1/3 cup chopped kale, stems removed

1/2 cup chopped fresh mango

1/2 cup chopped fresh papaya

1/2 cup frozen pineapple chunks

1/2 cup coconut water

4 ice cubes

RAW GREEN MACHINE SMOOTHIE

SERVES 2

1 leaf kale, stem removed

1 large green pear, chopped

1 small Granny Smith apple, sliced

½ small ripe banana

½ small cucumber, peeled and sliced

½ cup coconut water

Combine all ingredients in a blender and purée until smooth.

NUTRITIONAL INFORMATION Per Serving: 151 cal., 0 g fat, 0 g sat. fat, 39 g carb., 3 g protein, 80 mg sodium, 26 g sugar, 9 g fiber.

Raw Green Machine
Smoothie

SWEET PROTEIN-BOOST SMOOTHIE

SERVES 2

½ cup frozen strawberries

½ small ripe banana, peeled and sliced

½ cup low-fat milk (or substitute soy or almond milk)

1 tablespoon whey protein powder

Combine all ingredients in a blender and purée until smooth.

NUTRITIONAL INFORMATION Per Serving: 126 cal., 1 g fat, 1 g sat. fat, 15 g carb., 15 g protein, 70 mg sodium, 9 g sugar, 2 g fiber.

CHIA POWER SMOOTHIE

In a small bowl, stir together the chia seeds and 2 tablespoons water until a gel forms. Combine with the other ingredients in a blender and purée until smooth.

NUTRITIONAL INFORMATION Per Serving: 103 cal., 2 g fat, 0 g sat. fat, 22 g carb., 2 g protein, 2 mg sodium, 12 g sugar, 6 g fiber.

SERVES 2

1 tablespoon chia seeds

½ cup frozen raspberries

½ cup frozen strawberries

½ small ripe banana, peeled and sliced

½ cup apple juice (not from concentrate)

VITAMIN-C BOOST SMOOTHIE

SERVES 2

½ cup orange slices

½ cup pink grapefruit slices

½ cup frozen peaches

½ cup red apple slices

½ cup low-fat plain yogurt

4 ice cubes

Combine all ingredients with in a blender and purée until smooth.

NUTRITIONAL INFORMATION Per Serving: 114 cal., 1 g fat, 1 g sat. fat, 24 g carb., 5 g protein, 44 mg sodium, 20 g sugar, 3 g fiber.

DECLAN'S SIMPLE MORNING-DELIGHT SMOOTHIE

Combine all ingredients in a blender and purée until smooth.

NUTRITIONAL INFORMATION Per Serving: 150 cal., 2 g fat, 1 g sat. fat, 28 g carb., 7 g protein, 83 mg sodium, 26 g sugar, 1 g fiber.

SERVES 2

2 cups ripe watermelon, seeded and cut into chunks

1 cup low-fat vanilla yogurt

2 cups ice

SWEET-AND-HEARTY OATMEAL SMOOTHIE

SERVES 2

½ cup green or red apple slices

⅓ cup old-fashioned oatmeal, uncooked

⅓ cup vanilla yogurt

⅓ cup low-fat milk (or substitute unsweetened soy or almond milk)

⅛ teaspoon ground cinnamon

½ cup crushed ice

Combine all ingredients in a blender and purée until smooth.

NUTRITIONAL INFORMATION Per Serving: 119 cal., 2 g fat, 1 g sat. fat, 21 g carb., 3 g protein, 47 mg sodium, 11 g sugar, 2 g fiber.

WATERMELON SPRITZER SMOOTHIE

Combine all ingredients in a blender and purée until smooth.

NUTRITIONAL INFORMATION Per Serving: 52 cal., 0 g fat, 0 g sat. fat, 13 g carb., 1 g protein, 3 mg sodium, 10 g sugar, 1 g fiber.

SERVES 2

2 cups watermelon, seeded and cut into chunks

Juice of 1 lime

1 cup cold seltzer water

1 cup of ice

AVOCADO-PEAR BLITZ SMOOTHIE

SERVES 2

2 small pears, seeded, cored, chopped

½ small ripe avocado, peeled and chopped

1 tablespoon honey

½ teaspoon pure vanilla extract

6 ice cubes

Combine all ingredients a blender and purée until smooth.

NUTRITIONAL INFORMATION Per Serving: 198 cal., 14 g fat, 2 g sat. fat, 36 g carb., 3 g protein, 8 mg sodium, 25 g sugar, 14 g fiber.

BLOODY MARY WAKE-UP SMOOTHIE

Combine all ingredients in a blender and purée until smooth.

NUTRITIONAL INFORMATION Per Serving: 72 cal., 0 g fat, 0 g sat. fat, 14 g carb., 3 g protein, 208 mg sodium, 8 g sugar, 3 g fiber.

SERVES 2

1 cup loosely packed kale, stems removed

1 red pepper, cut into chunks

¼ cup peeled and sliced cucumber

1 stalk celery

1 cup low-sodium tomato juice

1 tablespoon lemon juice

1 tablespoon lime juice

½ tablespoon Worcestershire sauce

½ teaspoon hot sauce

6 ice cubes

CHOCOLATE AND STRAWBERRY SMOOTHIE

SERVES 2

1 cup fresh or frozen
   strawberries

½ cup low-fat vanilla yogurt

3 tablespoons semisweet
   chocolate chips

⅓ cup low-fat chocolate milk

4 ice cubes

Combine all ingredients in a blender and
purée until smooth.

NUTRITIONAL INFORMATION Per Serving: 195 cal.,
7 g fat, 5 g sat. fat, 31 g carb., 6 g protein, 67 mg
sodium, 26 g sugar, 2 g fiber.

SUPER GREEN SMOOTHIE

Combine all ingredients in a blender and purée until very smooth.

NUTRITIONAL INFORMATION Per Serving: 115 cal., 1 g fat, 0 g sat. fat, 19 g carb., 9 g protein, 128 mg sodium, 16 g sugar, 2 g fiber.

SERVES 2

1 Granny Smith apple, cored and coarsely chopped

2 cups baby spinach leaves

One 5.3-ounce container plain nonfat Greek Yogurt

1 cup light almond milk, chilled

2 teaspoons honey

DASH'S BERRY BLAST SMOOTHIE

SERVES 2

2 cups frozen strawberries
(or raspberries, blueberries,
or a combination)

1 very ripe banana, sliced

6 tablespoons nonfat vanilla
Greek yogurt

½ cup nonfat milk

Combine all ingredients in a blender and purée until smooth.

NUTRITIONAL INFORMATION Per Serving: 159 cal., 2 g fat, 0 g sat. fat, 36 g carb., 18 g protein, 188 mg sodium, 22 g sugar, 4 g fiber

MEASURE EQUIVALENTS CHART

Milliliters =	Teaspoons =	Tablespoons =	Fluid Ounces =	Cups =
15	3	1	.5	1/16
30	6	2	1	1/8
59	12	4	2	1/4
79	16	5	3	1/3
118	24	8	4	1/2
158	32	11	5	2/3
177	36	12	6	3/4
237	48	16	8	1

SIZE EQUIVALENCY CHART

Checkbook = 3-ounce serving of fish	**Shot glass =** 2 tablespoons of salad dressing	**Large egg =** ¼ cup of dried fruit or nuts
Four dice = 1 ounce of cheese	**Baseball =** 1 cup of raw leafy vegetables	**Compact disc =** Serving size of waffle or pancake
Tip of thumb = 1 teaspoon of peanut butter	**Computer mouse =** 1 serving of potato	**Lightbulb =** ½ cup of vegetables

INDEX